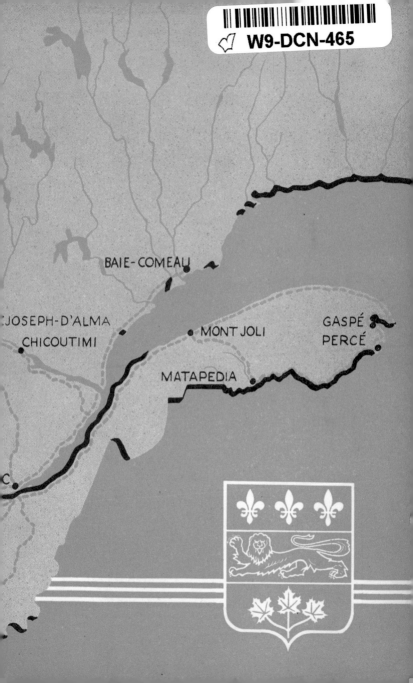

QUEBEC IN YOUR CAR

PROVINCIAL PARLIAMENT BUILDINGS, QUEBEC
Statues of famous Canadian heroes adorn the facade.

QUEBEC
IN YOUR CAR

by

JOHN AND MARJORIE MACKENZIE

Toronto
CLARKE, IRWIN & COMPANY LIMITED
1952

Printed in Canada

CONTENTS

Contents

ILLUSTRATIONS

Illustrations

All photographs in QUEBEC IN YOUR CAR are the
work of the authors.

FOREWORD

THOSE OF YOU who came with us for a tour of ONTARIO IN YOUR CAR know our way of travelling. We hope you will join us again on this new adventure, a motor tour through the Province of Quebec.

For our new readers, perhaps a word of explanation is in order. We want you to enjoy your holidays spent in Canada. We are sure you will have a wonderful time, if you know where to find the kind of holiday you are looking for. It is here, of that we are very sure, and we want to help you to find it.

If you will let us guide you, we promise to tell you the truth, as we see it. We shall take you to our favourite resorts, golf courses, ski runs, fishing and hunting grounds. We shall tell you, as we go, what we found of interest in each place.

In our opinion, sight-seeing is an art. It must be handled with subtlety and originality. It needs a touch of genius to keep it glowing and inspired. It can be ruined if it is laboured and over-done.

Sight-seeing, like any other fine art, is a pursuit in which the mind and the imagination must be engaged. The successful sight-seer keeps, at all times, a nice balance between the old and the new. He explores the country's ancient past with understanding, while he lives with pleasure in its modern present.

So pack your bags with comfortable clothes, leaving lots of room for the hooked rugs, wood carvings, and other handicraft articles you are sure to buy along the way. Bring a bathing suit for the lakes and pools of the mountain resorts and for the beaches on the sea. Bring your rods for the salmon fishing in the rivers of the

Gaspé, and your fly-rods and waders for the trout fishing in Laurentide Park. Have you ever caught a *ouananiche*? You can do that, too, in Lac St-Jean. For the hunting and fishing camps, you will need sturdy and warm camp clothing, and for the fashionable hotels at Murray Bay, Tadoussac, Montreal and Quebec, you will want your smartest attire.

Golfers, be sure to bring your clubs. There are interesting courses at most of the resorts, and in all the big cities. In the winter time, skis are standard equipment through the Laurentians, the Gatineau Hills and north of Quebec, and you won't find more exciting skiing anywhere.

If you do not like fishing, or golf, or skiing, come along anyway. There are wonderful sights to be seen, and the scenery up the Saguenay and around the Gaspé is as magnificent as any in the world.

History lives along these highways. The explorers and missionaries will come alive for you as you visit the places where they lived and worked. There is something for everyone, something for every season. We want to help you find your heart's desire.

You may come with us all the way, on our continuous trip through the whole province, or you may join us at any time, for a few days or a few miles. You may even, as many people do, stay home beside your fire, in a comfortable chair, and join us only in spirit.

Come, in your own way and at your own time, but do come. We are looking forward to having you with us, and we can promise you that Quebec will bid you a warm and hearty "Bienvenue".

JOHN AND MARJORIE MACKENZIE

Toronto
1952

Part One

THE PARIS OF NORTH AMERICA

Chapter 1

BIENVENUE—WELCOME

> ROAD LOG FOR HIGHWAY 2
> From the Ontario border to Montreal
>
> *Miles*
>
> **0** Ontario boundary line—Rivière-Beaudette
> **8** Coteau Landing
> **25** Dorion—Ile Perrot
> **29** Ste-Anne-de-Bellevue—Montreal Island
> **50** Montreal

OUR MOTOR TOUR of the Province of Quebec begins at an imaginary line, the border between the English-speaking province of Ontario and the French-speaking province of Quebec.

From time to time, people have tried to turn this boundary line into some kind of barrier. It is no barrier. It is not even a good sized hurdle, unless you are given to making mountains out of molehills. It may offer slight language difficulties, nothing more.

As we crossed the boundary on Highway 2, a road sign bid us **Bienvenue**, and we soon discovered that this is no empty word. By whatever road you enter, and from whatever corner of the world you may come, you will be warmly and sincerely welcome in La Province de Québec.

Quebec is Canada's largest province, territorially speaking. It has a total area of 594,860 square miles—almost three times the size of France. Its population of 4,000,000 is predominantly French in origin and in speech. Its largest city, Montreal, is Canada's biggest metropolis and ranks as the second largest French-speaking city in the world.

It was towards Montreal that we were heading as we crossed the boundary line and found ourselves at **Rivière-Beaudette** which means, in colloquial French-Canadian, the river with the narrow bed.

A moment before, in Ontario, we had been driving along the shore of Lake St. Francis. Now, we noticed, it was called Lac St-François.

You will soon get used to the idea that everything in Quebec has two names, one in English, the other in French.

A road sign warned us: "Gardez la droite—keep to the right". Other signs read: "Traverse—Ferry; École—School; Pont — Bridge; Stationnement interdit — No parking".

At the village of St-Zotique, a few miles farther along, a sign told us that there were: "Chaloupes à louer—Boats for rent".

We decided the only thing to do was to adopt the Quebec system of being bi-lingual. We hope you will do this too. It helps to know that "De la Montagne" and "Mountain Street" are one and the same; that "St. James Street" is apt to be called "Rue St-Jacques"; and that the "Fleuve St-Laurent" is the "St. Lawrence River". If you have forgotten nearly all your school book French, don't let it worry you. You will have little difficulty in making yourself understood. Even in the outlying villages where

4

English is seldom spoken, you will usually find someone who is willing and anxious to act as interpreter for you when your limited vocabulary fails. Don't be afraid to try. Don't be self-conscious or shy. We always carry a small French-English dictionary and look up a word if we can't remember it. If you do this, too, you will be amazed at how quickly your French will improve, especially when you are seeing and hearing it all around you.

At **Coteau Landing**, about 8 miles from the Ontario border, we came to the Soulanges Canal, part of the system of **canals around the rapids** of the St. Lawrence River. The locks between here and Lac St-Louis have a lift of 83 feet. Each lock is 280 feet long, 46 feet wide with a depth of water on the sills of 15 feet, large enough to permit ocean going vessels of 3,000 tons to pass up the river to the Great Lakes.

The *Prins Willem van Oranje* from Rotterdam was locking through as we passed, and presently we met the *Helfrid* of Göteborg coming up from Montreal. The highway runs along the bank of the canal for about fifteen miles, so close that the sailors and passengers waved to us as we passed, and we felt as if we, too, were on a boat.

All along this road there are **warning signs**: "Glissant si humide". These are not to be ignored, as the road is unusually slippery when wet, and it is necessary to drive slowly and with great care. Even if the road is dry, we hope you will not want to hurry too much. To feel the charm of the Soulanges Canal, and to see the beauty of the river scenery, a leisurely pace is most rewarding. We believe that most motor trips are ruined in a mad attempt to cover too many miles, too quickly.

From **Coteau-du-Lac** a **ferry** carries passengers and automobiles across the St. Lawrence River to Valleyfield, but we continued on Highway 2 into Montreal.

Already the picture was changing. No one can spend any time in Quebec without being impressed by the size and number of its **churches**. Everywhere they dominate the scene, and this very domination is, perhaps, the most significant and illuminating fact for strangers to grasp if they hope to understand the hearts and minds of the French Canadians.

You will see the new blue and white flag of the province flying, wherever there are French-speaking people. Its four white *fleurs de lis* represent the ancient ties with France, and its white cross is symbolic of the cross planted by Jacques Cartier, the French explorer, when he took possession of Canada more than four hundred years ago. The flag became the official emblem of La Province de Québec in 1948.

The Roman Catholic Church, the Provincial Flag, and the motto of Quebec: "*Je me souviens*—I remember." Therein lies the key to the French-Canadian ideology.

At **Pointe-aux-Cascades**, a good place to see the rapids in the river, the highway leaves the St. Lawrence and turns north to cross the Ottawa River on a bridge at Dorion.

Dorion (Population 2,000). This village is nicely placed on Vaudreuil Bay, overlooking Lac des Deux-Montagnes and the small village of **Vaudreuil**. The name Vaudreuil figures prominently in the history of the early days of the French colony on the island of Montreal, from the year 1687, when the Chevalier de Vaudreuil arrived from France to help defend the young colony against the incessant attacks of the Iroquois Indians, to the unhappy day for the French, in 1760, when the Marquis de Vaudreuil, the last Governor of New France, surrendered Montreal to the British. The name is remembered now, without much honour, in a small village, a bay, and a wayside inn.

In this area there are over-night cabins, a hotel and an **Auberge**. This is a word you will often see from now on. It means a hotel or inn. We found that an auberge was invariably run by French Canadians. Our French dictionary defines auberge as: "inn, public house, tavern," but the booklet of the Quebec Hotel Publications' describes an auberge as: "Type of quiet family hotel, of modest size, open all year. Moderate rates, no liquor license." An auberge it seems, like a château or a manoir or a chalet, is whatever the proprietor wishes to make it.

We crossed the bridge onto **Ile Perrot**, which divides the Ottawa River into two streams, and almost blocks the way between Lac St-Louis and Lac des Deux-Montagnes. As we drove along the wide concrete highway that crosses the northern end of Ile Perrot, we looked in vain for some remnant of the **storehouse and trading post** which Governor Perrot of Montreal built there in 1670 and which gave the island its name. It was part of Perrot's infamous scheme to divert the fur trade, for his own profit, before the Indians coming down the Ottawa River could reach the settlement at Montreal. To help him carry on this illegal trade, Perrot encouraged and protected a lawless band of *coureurs des bois*. For this, and other misdemeanours, he was put under arrest by Frontenac, tried at Quebec, and was imprisoned there for almost a year.

Frontenac also arrested one of Perrot's *coureurs des bois* and caused this unfortunate individual to be hanged in front of Perrot's prison window, no doubt to impress upon the Governor of Montreal the seriousness of his offence.

Perrot was then shipped to France for further punishment, but King Louis XIV evidently thought he had suffered enough for his sins. He released him after a few days imprisonment in the Bastille, and sent him back to Montreal as governor.

The bridge from Ile Perrot to the Island of Montreal crosses the Ottawa River at the historic and picturesque town of Ste-Anne-de-Bellevue.

Ste-Anne-de-Bellevue (Population 3,500) dates from the early days of the fur trade, and it was the place of departure for the *voyageurs* on their way up the Ottawa for the Grand Portage.

We turned off the highway and went down the hill to explore the old town. We particularly wanted to see **the house where Simon Fraser, the fur trader, used to live.** We found it on the narrow main street, almost in the shadow of the bridge. The old house is now occupied by the local branch of the Bank of Montreal, and we were delighted to see that it has been beautifully kept up, even to the white picket fence in front of it.

It was while he was staying in this house, in 1804, that the Irish poet, Thomas Moore, wrote the now famous Canadian Boat Song:

> Faintly as tolls the evening chime
> Our voices keep tune and our oars keep time.
> Soon as the woods on shore look dim,
> We'll sing at St. Ann's our parting hymn.

It was based on an old French song: *A l'ombre d'un bois je m'en vais jouer,* which the *voyageurs* sang as they rowed Moore from Kingston to Montreal. He wrote

(*Above*) THE HIGHWAY RUNS BESIDE THE CANAL
(*Below*) SIMON FRASER'S HOUSE AT STE-ANNE-DE-BELLEVUE

that the song recalled to his memory, "the dip of our oars in the St. Lawrence, the flight of our boat down the Rapids, and all those new and fanciful impressions to which my heart was alive during the whole of this very interesting voyage".

In a less poetic way, our hearts were alive, too, to the romance and beauty of this place, and we were tempted to linger. But already the "woods on shore looked dim", and Montreal, not Ste-Anne-de-Bellevue, was our destination for the night, so we returned to Route 2, a super-highway that leads from the bridge to the centre of the city, and drove on twenty miles to Montreal, **the Paris of America.**

Chapter 2

MONTREAL

ROAD LOG FOR HIGHWAYS
CONVERGING ON MONTREAL

Miles	*From*		*Highway*
350	Toronto, Ont. to Montreal		2
166	Quebec, P.Q. to	″	2
125	Ottawa, Ont. to	″	17
70	Malone, N.Y. to	″	4
97	Burlington, Vt. to	″	7
400	New York, N.Y. to	″	9

MONTREAL, CANADA'S LARGEST METROPOLIS, is **as gay and scintillating a city** as we have ever seen. It is sometimes called "The Paris of America", and the description fits it well. With a population of over a million and a half, it is unique in being **the largest bi-lingual centre in the world**. The paradox that has created Canadians and *Canadiens,* makes it necessary to say and to write everything twice, once in English and once in French.

We could not help smiling as we heard the elevator operators in the big shops singing out: "Second floor, *deuxième,* going down, please, *en bas, s'il vous plaît.*"

The last time we were in Montreal, we arrived on **St-Jean-Baptiste Day**, an annual provincial holiday in honour of the patron saint of the Province of Quebec. It is celebrated with street parades, bands, colourful floats and costumes, and ends with a magnificent display of fireworks in Lafontaine Park. Sherbrooke Street was so jammed with sight-seers that we could hardly find our way through the crowd to our hotel. It reminded us very much of the Mardi Gras parades of New Orleans, another old French colony that still clings to many of its ancient customs.

If you do not happen to like throngs of people milling about, and a city completely given over to a gay holiday spirit, you had better plan your visit to Montreal for some other date than the 24th of June.

The first thing to do is to find **a place to live**. It is not always easy. Long ago we adopted the system of writing or wiring ahead to Montreal for accommodations, and it is the safest way, especially if you have your heart set on staying at one particular place.

If you want to carry out the illusion of being in Paris, and if you are in an affluent mood and wish to see Montreal at its smartest, we think you will be delighted with the Ritz-Carlton Hotel. Like its namesake of the Place Vendôme in Paris, the Ritz of Montreal is a world-famous hostelry which needs no introduction from us. It is as fine as you are likely to find anywhere. In the summer there is **a charming cafe in the garden**, and at any time of year the service and appointments are note-worthy.

You will find the Ritz-Carlton Hotel on Sherbrooke Street (Highway 2) between Drummond and the street called either Mountain or De la Montagne.

Sherbrooke Street is **Montreal's longest highway**. It runs the entire length of the city, from Montreal West at its southern end to the north-eastern city limits. For a great many years it was the smartest and most fashion-able residential street. Now many of the Victorian mansions have been torn down and replaced by apart-

MONTREAL
(*Top*) Westmount Lookout. (*Middle*) The Windsor Hotel on Dominion Square.
(*Bottom*) The Ritz-Carlton Hotel on Sherbrooke Street.

ment houses; others have been transformed into offices and shops; some remain as private residences. It is still a beautiful street, with tall elms and maple trees on either side, and many handsome buildings and parks.

The question of where to stay has not been entirely settled. Your mood may be affluent, but not quite expansive enough to rise to the Ritz. In that case you might like the less famous and less expensive Berkeley Hotel, on the same side of Sherbrooke Street as the Ritz, one block east. Its **sidewalk cafe** is particularly nice on a warm summer evening. As it is called the Champs-Elysées, it furthers the illusion of being in Paris.

Farther away in spirit from the Rue de la Paix than either the Ritz or the Berkeley, but only a few blocks from them as actual distance goes, is another top-ranking hotel and a very popular one, the Mount Royal. You will find it on Peel Street, between Sherbrooke and St. Catherine. This is **Montreal's largest hotel** in the luxury class with 1100 rooms and baths, and it certainly is one of the gayest. We were particularly pleased with its Normandie Roof, which had a good orchestra for **dancing** the last time we were there, and a better than average **floor show**. Amazing as it may seem, the supper was delicious. It seemed to us to be a fine place for a colourful and syncopated holiday, if that is the sort of thing you like.

If it is not, you might prefer the sedate and slightly pompous Edwardianism of the Windsor Hotel, on Dominion Square. This is an old-timer but its present is as impressive as its past. The King and Queen were at the Windsor on their tour of Canada in 1939, and it was from the balcony of this hotel that they waved their greeting to the cheering crowds in the street below.

We like the Windsor's **big Edwardian bathrooms and**

its **large Victorian bedrooms**. Even its marble columns have a certain charm in this age of chromium plate and shiny tile. More leisurely and sedate than it needs to be, it still appeals to an older generation that has little love for the ultra modern.

Also on Dominion Square, across Dorchester Street from the Windsor, you will find the big, modernistic Laurentien Hotel, with over 1000 rooms. Its restaurant is run by the Murray chain. It offers **good value at popular prices** and its location is ideal.

Many people like the Hotel de La Salle, on Drummond Street, **a small, commercial hotel** with moderate rates. The old Queen's Hotel, farther down town on Windsor Street, still has a following.

Of the **guest houses**, we think the most pleasing are those on Pine Avenue West, near the top of Mountain Street.

All these places are in the centre of Montreal. If you can't get used to sleeping in a big city, but want to be near enough to come in and see the sights, you might like the Château Gai **Motel**, about ten miles from town. It is on the south side of the St. Lawrence River, best reached by the Mercier Bridge, and you will find it at the junction of Highways 3 and 4, not far from the village of Châteauguay. It is new and up-to-date, with a lounge, a dining room and a snack bar. Although it lacks the gaiety and romantic appeal of Montreal, it is a comfortable and reasonable overnight stop, and you can drive in to the city in half an hour or so.

Now that the problem of where to stay has been solved, we come to an even more important question.

Which are **the best restaurants?**"

In answering this one, we feel that we can throw aside our customary caution and indulge in a few superlatives.

We were delighted with the Café Martin, just around the corner from the Ritz-Carlton Hotel, at 1521 Mountain Street. There is a dining room on the main floor which serves a table d'hôte dinner, and in the high basement there is a grill room, specializing in sea food. The house itself, formerly a private residence, is interesting in its ornateness: white marble mantles; elaborately carved woodwork; colourful wall papers.

A menu doesn't mean much. It's the quality that counts. But we would like to tell you about the dinner we had at Café Martin for $2.00, and to assure you that every item was superb.

MENU

Hors-d'oeuvre

Crème soup - Jellied consommé

Salmon - sole - spaghetti

Roast lamb - Roast beef - Sweetbreads

Creamed spinach - Potatoes

Strawberries and Ice cream

Coffee

In the same class with Café Martin, and at about the same prices, we place Drury's **English Inn**, at the south side of Dominion Square. This is a very popular spot, and we had to wait for a table—but it was worth it.

Right up at the top of the list of restaurants is the Au 400 Café, one of our favourites. It occupies a handsome limestone house, set back from the street in a small garden, at 1490 Drummond Street. This place has **the piquancy of Paris**, and the good food and wines of that city, too. We spoke to the waiter in English. He answered, with apologies, in French. We came away with the happy feeling that we had dined well, and that Au 400 was distinctly Parisian.

Almost next door, at 1500 Drummond Street, you will

16

find another of our favourites, Chez Ernest. There is a suggestion of Italy in the fine quality of its spaghetti, but its French dishes are good, too. On the street level there is an entrance to the Colony Club. The main dining room is upstairs.

We are still flipping coins to decide which of the four is Montreal's finest restaurant: Café Martin, Drury's, Au 400 Café or Chez Ernest.

On a slightly less inspired level, **catering more to shoppers** and to business men, but very nice, too, is the restaurant on the 9th floor of Eaton's department store, on St. Catherine Street. It is spacious and pleasing, and after a lot of sight-seeing or shopping, it seems to be just right. The restaurant is open during store hours for lunch and tea. Eaton's is a branch of the T. Eaton Company's store in Toronto, one of the largest department stores in the world.

Another department store that has **a pleasing restaurant** is Morgan's, also on St. Catherine Street. We liked its Regency dining room, and particularly its cold buffet. On a hot day, the ice tables keep the salads crisp and appetizing. Nice for either lunch or tea, and the prices are moderate. Morgan's is a fine place to go shopping. Adjoining the dining room there is a comfortable sitting room and a most interesting gallery of antiques.

Montreal has **two unusual restaurants** which come under the heading of entertainment. They are distinct novelties, and you will probably want to visit them, if for no other reason than to talk about them when you get home.

The first is Au Lutin Qui Bouffe. It is at 753 St. Grégoire Street, and is quite hard to find. We finally tracked it down by driving east on Sherbrooke Street to

Lafontaine Park, where we turned left and kept going until we intersected St. Grégoire Street, about ten blocks northwest.

Au Lutin does not open its doors until 6 p.m., and it gets its large patronage mainly from tourists. There is organ or piano music, but no dancing. The interesting pictures about the walls were painted by some of the waiters. The chief entertainer is the tiny pink pig who is brought to each table to meet the guests, and to be photographed with them, if they wish it. On the way to your table you stop in the kitchen to choose your own steak. Not cheap, but an amusing evening.

Last on our list of interesting restaurants, and one that will delight you if you happen to like **Cantonese food**, is Ruby Foo's, "Canada's Largest Restaurant". It is on the outskirts of the city, at 7815 Décarie Boulevard, which the motorist will know better as Highway 11A.

There were at least a dozen Chinese recipes we had never heard of before, as well as all the old favourites. From ten o'clock until far into the night, Ruby Foo's presents **a musical revue** which puts it into the category of a night club. Expensive, but worth it if you are on a holiday and like that sort of thing.

A new "night spot" that shows signs of becoming popular is Leone's, on St. Catherine Street, which has a large dining room and bar. It is **a pleasant place to dine and dance**, without being too extravagant, and it remains open until 2 a.m.

There are literally dozens of fine restaurants in Montreal. We have only told you about our favourites, but we hope we have given you some idea of the variety there is from which to choose.

Now, having disposed of the important questions of where to sleep and eat, we can take time off to see the sights, to look at the beauties of Montreal, and to delve a bit into its colourful history.

Before you start off to see the city, your first call should be at the Provincial Tourist Bureau—*Service Provincial du Tourisme*—in the Dominion Square Building. It is open from 9 A.M. to 9 P.M., and they will give you a map of the city, illustrated booklets, and much useful information, in either English or French.

Probably the easiest way to see Montreal is to leave your car in the garage under the Dominion Square Building, walk to the Mount Royal Hotel or to the Windsor Hotel, and take one of the **guided tours** from there. Observation buses leave at frequent intervals, and for about $2.00 you can see the sights, once over lightly. Thousands of tourists see the city in this way each year.

It is the easiest way, but not necessarily the best way. When we tread on historic ground, or gaze at some magnificent scene, or wander through an impressive cathedral, we like to set our own pace. It jolts us out of the mood of a place to be hurried by a guide. If you feel that way about it, too, we suggest **a sight-seeing tour around Montreal in your own car** and at your own tempo.

Our tour begins where Montreal began. The mountain was there, according to some geologists, over sixty million years ago. At that time it was about 3,000 feet high, but the erosion of the ages has worn it down to its present height of 750 feet.

The history of Montreal begins at the foot of this mountain, near the present gates of McGill University, on Sherbrooke Street. According to a Memorial Stone placed there in 1925, this was where Jacques Cartier discovered the Indian town of Hochelaga in 1535.

It usually requires patience and a lot of imagination to bring back famous people from the past, and to reconstruct the world around them as it was when they lived in it. Jacques Cartier has saved us this effort by describing in detail what he found when he arrived at the place now known as Montreal.

In his *Relation Originale* he tells us how he and his companions landed, one October day, on the shore of the St. Lawrence, and how the Indians welcomed them by dancing far into the night. He tells us that he followed a well-worn path for about two miles to the foot of the mountain and found there a stockaded settlement of at least fifty dwellings, which was called Hochelaga.

Cartier read to the Indians from the Gospel of St. John: "In the beginning was the Word, and the Word was with God, and the Word was God."

Obviously, the savages could not understand the Word, but they listened in silence, with marvellous attention, rolling their eyes up to heaven and imitating the gestures of the Frenchmen.

From this story it is evident that, when discovered by Cartier, the Indians of Hochelaga were friendly, co-operative and quite willing to learn the white man's ways.

After naming the high hill Mont-Réal, Jacques Cartier and his companions departed, and no more was ever heard or seen of Hochelaga. Either it was burnt, or the Indians moved away—historians are divided on the question—but not one of the later explorers mentions the place.

Let us follow Jacques Cartier and his sailors back to their boats on the St. Lawrence River. Leaving Hochelaga, they may have gone down what is now University, along Dorchester to Beaver Hall Street, and down the hill to Victoria Square. There were no **one-way streets** to bother them in 1535, but today you will have to keep a careful watch for the **direction arrows**. In Montreal, one-way streets change from hour to hour, with the rush-hour traffic. If you want to avoid all traffic and parking problems, do your exploring on Sunday.

At Victoria Square, where Craig Street intersects it, you will be standing on the threshold of Ville-Marie, **the old walled and fortified town** which was the beginning of Montreal. The birthplace of Ville-Marie was at the Place Royale, which you will find by going down McGill Street and along Youville Square. It faces the harbour and Alexandra Pier, on Commissioners Street.

And now we may wave good-by to Jacques Cartier and his men, as they sail away down the river, and we may wait to welcome the coming of Samuel de Champlain, the next recorded historical event at Mont-Réal.

It will be a long wait, because sixty-eight years elapsed before the famous French explorer broke the silence of this island by landing from his shallop. The ferocity of the Grand Sault (Lachine Rapids) barred his further journey upstream.

Champlain's landing place was the original Port of Montreal. In those early days the river came right up to Commissioners Street. A small island, later to be known as Ilot Normandin, gave shelter to the boats. The island is now buried under the harbour piers.

Champlain was evidently impressed with the place, because he came back, eight years later, and laid out a trading post and settlement, which he called Place Royale. He was pleased with the fine meadows, where once the Indians of Hochelaga had grown their corn. He was well satisfied with the fruit trees, the fish and the game birds. He built a storehouse and dwelling, and sent out messengers to the Indians to tell them that he was ready to trade. They came with their beaver skins, in June 1611. So began the commercial life of Canada's largest city.

With the fur trade came distrust and much talk of Indian wars. Champlain had taken sides with the Hurons against the Iroquois, and had thereby earned the hatred of that powerful tribe. From this time on the story of Montreal is a tale of fear of the Iroquois, of horrors and massacres, and of a continuous struggle for self-preservation.

Champlain was by nature an explorer, not a trader. After two months he left Place Royale to continue his famous voyages of discovery, and although he often passed this way, he never again lived at Mont-Réal.

Thirty-one years elapsed before the coming of Maisonneuve and his permanent settlers. While we are waiting for them, suppose we look at the **Place Royale** as it is today. A small patch of grass, hemmed in by stone buildings and railroad tracks and the warehouses of the harbour. You could miss it altogether if it were not for **the odd stone obelisk** that rises thirty feet high in the centre of the square. It is worn and weather-beaten. Its four bronze tablets tell the story in French of the founding of Montreal.

Champlain is given some credit for the part he played, but Paul de Chomedy, Sieur de Maisonneuve is accepted by Montreal as its founder. The date of the founding is given as the eighteenth of May, 1642, and the place as Champlain's Place Royale, which thereafter became known as Ville-Marie de Montréal.

If you take your map of present-day Montreal and draw a line on it from Place Royale along Commissioners Street to Berri, up Berri to Craig Street—which was a marshy river in the early days—along Craig and down

MONTREAL
(*Above*) Champlain's Place Royale as it is today.
(*Below*) Château de Ramezay, built in 1705.

McGill to Common Street, and from there back to Place Royale, you will have outlined the limits of Ville-Marie. Within this area, behind the walls and fortifications against the hostile Iroquois, the mission settlement grew into the city of Montreal.

Before we leave Place Royale to explore the narrow streets and the ancient buildings, let us pause at the obelisk to welcome Paul Chomedy, Sieur de Maisonneuve and his gallant company as they sail into port. They have been sent from France by the newly formed Associates of Notre-Dame de Montréal, and they have come, not to trade in furs with the Indians but "to promote the glory of God and the salvation of the savages."

It is a May morning, in the year 1642. With Maisonneuve is the courageous Jeanne Mance, who has come to establish a hospital for the Indians; Madame de La Peltrie, from the Ursuline convent at Quebec; Father Poncet and the Jesuits who hope to build a mission and seminary to convert the savages to Christianity; Father Vimont from the mission at Quebec; and about fifty others, carpenters, weavers, shoemakers and labourers.

As soon as they land they will fall on their knees in prayer, and when they have built an altar, the first Mass of Ville-Marie will be celebrated, here at Place Royale. And now we can continue our tour of Montreal, knowing that it has been founded in faith.

Immediately behind the Place Royale you will find the city's oldest thoroughfare, called St. Paul Street. Up a short laneway, within a stone's throw of the obelisk, you can stand on the foundations of **Maisonneuve's house**. It was remodelled to become the first Séminaire de Saint-Sulpice when, in 1663, the lands and obligations of the Company of the Associates of Montreal were transferred to that religious order, making them the feudal owners of the Island of Montreal, by consent of King Louis XIV of France.

Here, then, is the heart and core of the earliest history of the city, here in a lane off St. Paul Street. A plaque placed there by the *Commission des Monuments Historiques* is inscribed in French, and reads in translation:

IN 1663
THE GENTLEMEN OF SAINT-SULPICE
CONSTRUCTED HERE THEIR FIRST
RESIDENCE IN CANADA
M. DE MAISONNEUVE
FOUNDER OF MONTREAL
LIVED HERE UNTIL HIS DEPARTURE
FROM THE COLONY IN 1665

A trail led from Maisonneuve's house to the first public building erected by the settlers, Jeanne Mance's hospital, called the Hôtel-Dieu. The trail became Rue St-Paul, the leading residential and business street of Ville-Marie. Jeanne Mance's hospital stood for fifty years at the corner of St. Paul and St. Sulpice Streets. It opened its doors to the sick and wounded just two years after the landing of the colonists.

As you walk along St. Paul Street you will notice that many of the buildings are marked with historic plaques, giving the location of the early houses, and the names of the colonists who lived in them. A name you will recognize is that of Le Moyne. Charles Le Moyne de Longueuil and his eleven sons have filled pages of Canadian and American history. For services to the colony, King Louis XIV knighted Charles and gave him the Seigneurie of Longueuil, across the river from Montreal. Two of his many sons, d'Iberville and de

Bienville, were the founders of Louisiana, where de Bienville lived as governor for thirty-five years. The oldest son, Charles Le Moyne de Longueuil became Governor of Montreal in 1724 and provisional Governor of Canada the following year.

If you will go up St. Sulpice Street to Notre-Dame, it will bring you to the **Place d'Armes**, a city square which is as important today as it was three hundred years ago, where **a handsome monument** to Paul Chomedy, Sieur de Maisonneuve, was erected in 1892. There he stands, a fine figure dressed in the plumes and satins of a gentleman of 1642, proudly holding an old French flag. Among the figures at the base of the monument are those of Jeanne Mance, caring for a wounded Indian child, and of Charles Le Moyne, Baron de Longueuil. The monument is the work of the famous Quebec sculptor, Philippe Hébert.

The Place d'Armes is surrounded by some of Montreal's most interesting buildings, the oldest and most historic of which is the **Séminaire de Saint-Sulpice**. This is the "new" seminary, built between 1685 and 1712, on property adjoining the old seminary in Maisonneuve's house on the Place Royale. There is a sombre dignity to its rough grey stone walls, the only ornament being a quaint square clock set in the roof above the front door.

The gigantic and colourful figure of Dollier de Casson, explorer, soldier and priest, is closely connected with this seminary. When he retired from his voyages of exploration and discovery, he came back to live in Montreal, and to write its history, in 1674. He laid out the streets of the growing town, and was the first to plan a canal around the Lachine Rapids. He became the Superior of the Sulpicians. A tablet on the seminary wall commemorates him:

FRANÇOIS DOLLIER DE CASSON,
FIRST HISTORIAN OF MONTREAL
CAPTAIN UNDER MARSHAL DE TURENNE
THEN PRIEST OF SAINT-SULPICE FOR 35 YEARS
HE DIED IN 1701, CURÉ OF THE PARISH

With the death of Dollier de Casson in 1701 we leave behind the name of Ville-Marie de Montréal. From now on the place is known simply as Montreal.

Quebec is a province of magnificent churches, but there is one among them that lingers in our memories. It is **the parish church of Montreal**, next to the Séminaire de Saint-Sulpice. Even if it is not part of your usual sight-seeing programme to visit old churches, we hope you will make an exception for this one.

Notre-Dame de Montréal is the direct descendant of the first rude chapel erected by Maisonneuve and his followers in 1642. The present impressive church, built of local limestone, was begun in 1824 and was opened for public worship five years later. The two square towers, rising to a height of two hundred and fifteen feet, dominate the Place d'Armes. The Tower of Perseverance houses the *Gros Bourdon*, an enormous bell weighing over twenty-four thousand pounds. The Tower of Temperance contains the chimes.

The interior of the church is magnificent, with an unusual double row of galleries around the nave, which is two hundred and twenty feet in length and can hold more than twelve thousand people. But it is not the size of Notre-Dame that makes it memorable. It is its dignity, its history, and its unusual beauty.

Across the Place d'Armes, facing the church and the Seminary of Saint-Sulpice, you will see **a handsome stone building** of classical design, with Corinthian columns and Roman dome. It is the head office of the

Bank of Montreal, one of the city's oldest financial institutions. Today it has over five hundred branches in Canada. The present building was erected a little more than a century ago, in 1848, but the bank was established in 1817, the same year that saw the last of the walls and fortifications which surrounded the old city.

Before we progress too far in time, let us go out Notre Dame Street and explore the rest of the **historic buildings.**

You will probably find it rather confusing, as we did, to be told to go east on Notre Dame Street, when the street runs almost north and south. Montrealers speak of going north on Côte des Neiges Road, which actually runs from east to west. It is one of the oddities of Montreal's lay-out, but once you learn that east means north and north means west it is all quite simple.

In local parlance, go east on Notre Dame Street, past the new and old court houses, to the massive and imposing **City Hall.** These are all nineteenth century buildings which impressed us with their Victorian elegance, but they do not belong in our historical tour.

Directly opposite the City Hall, and somewhat dwarfed by it, is the **Château de Ramezay,** built as a private residence in 1705. We think it gives a very good idea of how the town had grown and prospered during the sixty-three years since Maisonneuve and his settlers first landed at the Place Royale.

Park your car and go inside. It is open as **a museum,** from 10 A.M. until 5 P.M. on week days, and on Sunday afternoon, from 2 until 5. It has a varied and interesting story, and it is one building we are sure you will not want to miss.

When Claude de Ramezay built the house, it stood at the northern town limits, in spacious grounds, overlooking the St. Lawrence River. Because de Ramezay was the Governor of Montreal, we can assume that it was the centre of the social life of the place. Today its grounds have shrunk to almost nothing, and it seems crowded and jostled by the busy city all around it, but within its walls something of the old spirit remains.

It was used for a time as a fur trading post, after Claude de Ramezay's death in 1724. With the close of the French regime in Canada, the Château was bought by the British Government for two thousand guineas and became Government House.

Its most colourful period was at the time of the American Revolution. Benedict Arnold used it as his headquarters in 1776. In the spring of that year, about two months before the American Declaration of Independence, Benjamin Franklin came to Montreal and to the Château de Ramezay, with his famous Congressional Mission. He came in the hope that Canada might be persuaded to become the fourteenth state of the new United States of America. Charles Carroll of Maryland was with him, reputed to be the richest man in America in his day. As you walk through the old house, perhaps you will be able to visualize Benjamin Franklin and Charles Carroll and the other distinguished members of the Commission being entertained at a fashionable reception on their arrival in the city. Perhaps you can also visualize Fleury Mesplet working at the printing press set up in the basement of the Château for the purpose of printing what we would call nowadays anti-British Propaganda.

But it did not succeed. The Commission was a complete failure, although one good thing came of it. When the others returned to the United States, Mesplet, the printer, remained behind to produce Montreal's first newspaper, *La Gazette,* in 1778. Ten years later it became bilingual, and eventually it turned into the city's leading English language morning paper.

One could spend hours in the Château de Ramezay, looking over the old prints and letters, the books and coins, the furniture and other mementoes of the French regime. The collection is noteworthy. We do not want to hurry you away. See it all at your leisure, and when you are ready, leave the old Château to its interesting past and wander down the hill behind it to **one of Montreal's most colourful corners.**

Here, near the Jacques Cartier Square, we come again upon St. Paul Street—the same street that runs behind the Place Royale. At the corner of St. Paul and St. Claude Streets, the period changes abruptly from old French to early Victorian. The massive stone building of Greek classical revival architecture with the heavy Doric columns is **the Marché Bonsecours, the market place** for more than a hundred years. In its earliest days it was used as the City Hall, and many fashionable concerts and banquets were held in the rooms on the second floor.

Across the street from the market, was Montreal's smartest hotel, the famous Rasco's, which opened its doors in 1835 and remained in favour for many years. England's immortal novelist Charles Dickens, and his wife Kate, stayed at Rasco's Hotel on their visit to Canada in 1842. On that occasion, Dickens made his debut as an actor by appearing in several plays put on by the officers of the garrison at the old Theatre Royal, which stood just around the corner on Bonsecours Street. Rasco's Hotel has vanished from the scene, although the building remains.

Just beyond the market is a link with the more remote past, **the Church of Notre-Dame-de-Bonsecours**. Its

MONTREAL
(*Above*) Our Lady of Good Help blesses the boats.
(*Below*) Beyond the market is a link with the past—the Church of
Notre-Dame-de-Bonsecours.

foundations date from 1657. It was almost half a century old when the Château de Ramezay was built. Maisonneuve gave the land for it when Montreal was still Ville-Marie. The church was inspired by the beloved Marguerite Bourgeoys, who joined the mission colony in 1653 to become its teacher, and whose work is still carried on by the Sisters of the Congregation of Notre-Dame. She brought with her to Ville-Marie money to build a chapel.

For almost three hundred years this Church of Notre-Dame-de-Bonsecours has been **a sanctuary for seamen**. From above the chapel, the statue of Our Lady of Good Help blesses the boats and the sailors as they leave the harbour. Fire destroyed much of the earlier building, and the present church dates mostly from 1771. When you go inside be sure to look at the tile mosaics which commemorate the founders of the church— Marguerite Bourgeoys and Maisonneuve.

Now we have come to the end of the old city. Beyond the Church of Notre-Dame-de-Bonsecours is Berri Street, where the walls and fortifications guarded the early settlement from Indian attacks.

This is a good time to investigate **Montreal's interesting harbour,** for just behind the Bonsecours Church you will find Victoria Pier, where you may park your car and **take an excursion boat for a 25 mile trip around the water front and down the river**. It is a good way to get a closer view of the ocean-going ships. Our boat left at 2.30 in the afternoon, but as **schedules** are **subject to change without notice**, it would be wise to enquire about sailing time before going down to the pier. Several boats make these river trips. Ours was the Motor Vessel *Ville Marie* of the Chester Lines. She was a pleasant, small, excursion boat with a snack bar for drinks and sandwiches. At night there was **a searchlight cruise, when the main deck was given over to dancing**.

As we left Victoria Pier, we could see towering above us the enormous statue of Notre-Dame-de-Bonsecours, atop her church, with arms outstretched to bless the ships and all who sail therein.

The Captain of the *Ville Marie* kept up a running commentary in both French and English, which was broadcast to the passengers through loud speakers. He told us that the clock tower at the end of Victoria Pier was a memorial to the sailors who died in the First Great War. He said that the island in the centre of the river was named Ile Ste-Hélène by Champlain, in honour of his child wife, and that it was now a city park. He explained that the bridge spanning the river across this island was the Jacques Cartier Harbour Bridge, built in 1930, and that the old bridge, two miles upstream was officially opened in 1860 by King Edward VII, then Prince of Wales, and named Victoria Bridge in honour of the Queen, his mother. As we came close to the ocean liners in the port, he told us that one was the *Athelmere* with molasses from the West Indies, and that another was the passenger ship *Ascania* from London. He named each ship in this enormous harbour, giving her home port and her cargo. He even gave us a brief history of Montreal, beginning with the founding of Ville-Marie by Maisonneuve. Altogether, he was an amazing source of information.

Our cruise lasted three hours, took us as far down the river as Pointe-aux-Trembles, near the foot of Montreal Island, and gave us a comprehensive view of Canada's largest port, which is second only to New York on the North American continent.

If you are in the right mood, and have just a touch

of the "tripper" spirit, we are sure you will enjoy one of the river cruises.

Enough is enough when it comes to sight-seeing, and after a day spent exploring the old city and the harbour, you will probably be ready for one of Montreal's fine French restaurants, and after that, perhaps, a theatre, a night club, or bed. Tomorrow is another day, and there are still many things to see and to do.

If, when you wake in the morning, it is a rainy day, you might plan a visit to the **Montreal Art Gallery**, at 1379 Sherbrooke Street. The Art Association of Montreal has gathered together a fine collection of paintings and art treasures, housed in a charming building which is open daily from 10 until 5, and from 2 until 5 on Sundays.

If, however, the day is clear and sunny, this would be a good time to explore the modern city and to see the spectacular view from **the Lookout**. A good place to begin this sight-seeing tour is at **McGill University**, on Sherbrooke Street, where we began the historical tour of the old city. This time, we shall go north and west. McGill, one of Canada's oldest and most famous universities, was founded according to the terms of the Will of James McGill, a Montreal fur trader and magistrate, who died in 1813. It was thirty years later before the first buildings were completed and the first classes held. At that time the enrolment was twenty students. Now it is over eight thousand. The founder is commemorated in the students' song:

> Peacefully he slumbers there,
> Though he knows we're on the tear.
> He's our father
> Oh yes, rather,
> James McGill.

We found the drive around the mountain interesting. From McGill University we drove up Park Avenue, then along Côte Ste-Catherine (not to be confused with the shopping street of the same name). This road winds its way through the incorporated city of **Outremont** ("beyond the mountain") an attractive residential section of Greater Montreal.

When we were half way around Mount Royal, we saw the huge modernistic buildings of the **Université de Montréal** towering high above us. They are reputed to have over six miles of corridors. For a closer view, drive along Mount Royal Boulevard, which goes through the grounds.

Not far from the Université de Montréal, and vying with it for domination of the skyline, you will see **Saint Joseph's Oratory**, one of Montreal's most spectacular buildings. It is on Queen Mary Road, near the corner of Côte des Neiges.

This **world-famous shrine** stands on the slope of Westmount Mountain, and rises to an impressive height of more than 500 feet. Pilgrims come by the thousands every day. Each sight-seeing bus, each guided tour, pauses here to see this monument to the humble door-keeper and school messenger, Brother André, the "miracle man of the mountain", whose faith and devotion made it possible.

Across the street, in the **Musée Historique Canadien**, there is a remarkably life-like wax figure of Brother André, made fifteen years ago, when he was 92 years old. It is only one of a collection of life-size wax figures which depict the story of Christianity and of the early days of Montreal in a realistic manner. We think it is well worth a visit.

Drive back towards town on Côte des Neiges, but be sure to turn off on Belvedere Road to take the Summit Circle around Westmount Lookout.

Like Outremont, **Westmount** is a separately incorporated city with a population of 30,000. It is entirely surrounded by Montreal, and it comprises one of the most beautiful and fashionable residential areas. Park your car at **Westmount Lookout**. On a clear day, you can see the whole panorama of the city, with the distant Green Mountains of Vermont far beyond.

Even more spectacular is the **Lookout on Mount Royal**, but to see this you must walk, or take one of the **horse-drawn carriages**, as no motor vehicles are allowed in Mount Royal Park. This beautiful, natural mountain park, which covers almost five hundred acres, was laid out one hundred years ago to be preserved in perpetuity.

In the summertime there are **outdoor theatrical performances** given in this lovely setting, and during July and August you can hear **symphony concerts** played **under the stars**.

In the winter, the whole place becomes a playground, with **a toboggan slide, and a ski club** for visitors.

A giant Cross on the summit of the mountain, brilliantly lighted at night, shines forth over the city and the countryside. Symbolic of the faith in which Ville-Marie was founded, it occupies the place of the wooden cross, planted on this same hill, in 1643, by Maisonneuve.

Mount Royal is the most impressive of the parks, but it is by no means the only one. If you are a golfer or a tennis player, you will enjoy the **Parc Maisonneuve**. You will find it by going north and east on Sherbrooke Street (Route 2) through what is known as the French section of the city. On the way you will pass **Parc Lafontaine and the Montreal Public Library**.

SAINT JOSEPH'S ORATORY, MONTREAL
Pilgrims come by the thousands.

The Parc Maisonneuve covers almost three hundred acres and contains the **Botanical Gardens** and the **Municipal Golf Course**. This is a well maintained full length course, par 72, open to the public. There are, also, 18 tennis courts, and a club house with lockers.

Altogether there are **more than twenty golf courses on the Island of Montreal**. Most of the best clubs are private, and it is necessary to be put up by a member, but if you have come to Montreal with the idea of playing golf, you will find several public courses within easy motoring distance of your hotel. We like the Mount Royal Golf Club, in the town of Mount Royal, beyond Outremont, and the La Salle Golf and Country Club, which has a charming setting beside the Lachine Rapids of the St. Lawrence River. Both clubs allow visitors to play on payment of a daily fee.

If it is **spectator sports** you are looking for, Montreal has everything, according to the season. **Baseball** is played by teams of the International League at the Stadium on Delorimier Avenue, in the east end of the city, not far from the Parc Lafontaine. The **racing** season draws enthusiasts from all over the country to the Blue Bonnets Race Course on Décarie Boulevard, (Highway 11A) almost opposite Ruby Foo's restaurant.

When autumn comes, the "Big Four" **football** games are played to enthusiastic crowds in the Molson Stadium, at McGill University, on Pine Avenue near Park. And in the winter time you can see "The World's Fastest Game", played by the world's fastest teams, on the home ice of **the Montreal Canadiens** in the huge Forum on St. Catherine Street West.

The daily newspapers carry accounts of all the sporting events, and tell you where and when you can see them. The concerts, theatres, and other amusements are also advertised daily, and if there is anything more you want to know about Montreal, remember the Provincial Tourist Bureau on Dominion Square is there to serve you.

So far, in our sight-seeing jaunts around town, we have covered only the central area. Now we would like to take you for a drive around the island and across the river, a scenic tour too interesting to miss.

Chapter 3

AROUND THE ISLAND OF MONTREAL

ROAD LOG FOR HIGHWAY 37
AROUND MONTREAL ISLAND

Miles

0	Montreal - Dominion Square
3	Verdun
7	Lachine Rapids
9	Mercier Bridge
10	La Salle
13	Lachine
15	Dorval
22	Pointe-Claire
29	Ste-Anne-de-Bellevue
32	Senneville
37	Ste-Geneviève
38	Ile Bizard Bridge
46	Belmont - Bridge to Ile Jésus
50	Montréal-Nord
61	Bout-de-l'Ile (End of the Island)
66	Pointe-aux-Trembles
78	Montreal

ONE OF THE SURPRISING THINGS about Montreal is the ease with which you can leave the bustle of big business and find yourself, in a few short miles, in fascinating lake and river country, with lovely scenery and many of the attractions of more distant holiday resorts.

It would be a pity to leave this area without taking

the drive around the Island of Montreal. **Highway 37 completely circles the island** and it is a good road most of the way. Occasionally it is winding and narrow, but there is not much traffic on it now, since the building of the wide super-highways, and we found it a delightful drive.

Our first and biggest surprise was to find the third largest city in the province immediately adjoining Montreal on the southwest.

Verdun (Population 70,000) began its life as a somewhat slummy site for factories and an asylum, but it has matured and grown into a pleasant and well-balanced industrial city. We walked on its two mile long **Boardwalk** at Riverside Park. Beside us was a tennis club, all the courts in play. Below us, along the river front, hundreds of small boats were moored. Other boats were speeding about in the sheltered water between the Park and Nun's Island, which you will see in the St. Lawrence River, opposite Verdun. It is a large island, with about five hundred acres of farmland. The Community House of Our Lady of Protection, run by the Sisters of the Congregation of Notre-Dame, is the original building dating from 1788.

We continued our drive along La Salle Boulevard, which follows closely the early trail between the La Salle Seigneurie, near Lachine, and old Ville-Marie. At **La Salle**, just beyond Verdun, there is a fascinating view of **the Lachine Rapids**, the swiftly running water swirling and splashing around many small islands, and the scenery on shore matching it in beauty. Lush green trees, growing to the river's edge, screen out all signs of industry. You can easily imagine that you are miles away in the country, especially when you look across the road and find there the La Salle Golf and Country Club. It has a regular membership, predominantly French Canadian, but it welcomes visitors, who may play its 18 hole course on payment of the usual greens fee.

At the western end of the Seigneurie which was granted to the great explorer, Robert Cavelier de La Salle, in the year 1668, there is a good place to pause for a moment, mentally and physically. You will find **a parking lot** beside the river.

Across the road is the **old house** sometimes known as "The La Salle House" but now conceded to have been built by Charles Le Moyne of Longueuil, between the years 1670 and 1680. A legend persists that the chimney of this house was built by Champlain. However that may be, the place is steeped in history.

The old house is now **a museum**. Built with the French-colonial high pitched roof, the architectural lines are sound as well as graceful.

It was from this seigneurie that the La Salle expedition started forth in 1669 to find a way to China. Tradition has it that the name *La Chine* was given later, as a term of derision, but in his contemporary *History of Montreal* 1640-1672, Dollier de Casson of the Séminaire de St-Sulpice mentions the place several times as *la Chine*. He refers to it as "un endroit vulgairement *la Chine*" as early as 1643. Again, in a humorous vein, he wrote of the transmigration to China in 1667, explaining that it would be "very consoling for those who are coming to Mont Royal to learn that it is only three leagues from China", (qu'il n'est qu'à trois lieues de la Chine.)

In the garden of the old house, the Provincial Government has started **a fish hatchery for maskinonge**, which was in the experimental stages when we saw it, but promised to grow into something quite interesting.

VERDUN

(*Above*) Hundreds of small boats were moored at Riverside Park.
(*Below*) The Lachine Rapids.

A mile or so beyond, we crossed **the Lachine Canal**, which extends from Lac St-Louis to Montreal Harbour, a distance of a little less than nine miles. There are always a great many boats coming and going in the canal, as all vessels going up or down the river must pass this way.

In the early days of Ville-Marie, Dollier de Casson had plans for such a canal, and considerable work was done on it before 1689, as even in those days of small bateaux and canoes the rapids were a great barrier to navigation. But progress on the canal was slow, due to lack of money and to hostility to the scheme in France, so that when Dollier de Casson died in 1701 only about two thirds of the canal had been cut, and he had spent over twenty-thousand livres on the project.

It was more than a hundred years later, in 1825, before the Lachine Canal was opened. Through the years since then it has grown to its present importance and capacity.

If boats interest you, you will see them here, of all kinds and sizes. Small privately owned cruisers and ocean-going freighters from foreign countries use this canal on their way through to the Great Lakes.

Lachine (Population 21,000). After you have crossed the canal, you will find yourself in the city of Lachine, a pleasant place with **a yacht club and a canoe club** on Lac St-Louis, and with several **golf courses** within a radius of a few miles, including the 18 hole Meadowbrook Golf Club, where visitors may play.

Lachine began its life in 1667 as a fur trading post, and became the port of embarkation for bateaux and canoes travelling west. It grew with the building of the canal, and by 1847 it became the terminus of the first

THE LA SALLE SEIGNEURIE
The old house is now a museum.

railway on the Island of Montreal, The Montreal and Lachine Railway, now part of the C.N.R.

Its darkest hour was in August 1689, when fifteen hundred Iroquois Indians landed at Lachine, surrounded the houses along the shore and, at a signal, began the massacre of the inhabitants. It was part of a prepared plan to wipe out French Canada. Eighty soldiers guarding the village and two hundred men, women and children were killed, and one hundred and twenty were taken away as prisoners, to be tortured and burned at the stake.

A monument has been erected on La Salle Boulevard to the victims of the Massacre of Lachine.

Probably no pages of history have been written with such one-sided prejudice as the stories of the Indian wars, and of the tortures and atrocities the savages inflicted on the early settlers in Canada and the United States. The tortures were unspeakably horrible, but to see the thing in its proper perspective we should remember that the raids were often reprisals, as was the massacre of Lachine. Denonville, then Governor of New France, had sent 51 Indians to work as galley slaves in France, and had made repeated attacks on the Iroquois, burning their villages and laying waste their lands, in the hope of bringing the savages to submission. We should remember, also, that at the same period of history civilized Christian men in many parts of the world were burning white women at the stake on the thin excuse that they were witches. Perhaps the Iroquois thought that they, too, were burning witches. Who knows? We do not propose to take sides in this age-old argument. We merely want to try and see the thing in its true light.

A stone post marks the division between Lachine and

Dorval, but no other dividing line is apparent as you drive along Highway 37.

Dorval (Population 2,500). The two courses of the Royal Montreal Golf Club (Dixie), and the Elm Ridge Country Club are nearby, and five other courses are within a few miles of the town. On a point of land, within the shelter of Dorval Island, you will see the **Royal St. Lawrence Yacht Club**, and beyond it the beautiful open reaches of Lac St-Louis, much used for sailing. A road goes right to the Dorval Traffic Circle, on Highways 2 and 17, and leads to the **Municipal Airport** of Montreal.

For the next few miles the road follows the shore of the lake, passing some charming country places and many quaint old cottages reminiscent of the French regime.

Pointe-Claire (Population 5,000). This residential suburb might almost be called a **summer resort**. The Yacht Club was having a sailing race with about fifty entries, when we were there in June. The Beaconsfield **Golf Club** adjoins the town. Beyond this is real country, with a few farms and more widely scattered houses.

Ste-Anne-de-Bellevue (Population 3,500). Like most of the cities, towns and villages on the Island of Montreal, this one began as a fur trading post, in 1670, about the time that the stone house was being built on the La Salle Seigneurie, and the same year that saw the arrival from France of François Perrot, to be Governor of Montreal. It continued as a fur trading centre for about two hundred years. Simon Fraser was in charge of the post belonging to the North West Company, that great rival of the Hudson's Bay Company, and if you have not already seen his house, at 153 St. Anne Street, you will be glad to know that the Ste-Anne-de-Bellevue Branch of the Bank of Montreal, which now occupies it, "is always pleased to welcome visitors and to show them the historic building."

In passing, you might also like to see the interesting campus and buildings of the **Macdonald Agricultural College**, affiliated with McGill University.

We think the road is particularly pretty after you pass under the bridge from Ile Perrot and drive along the tree-shaded country lane through Gardenvale and Senneville. The lake here is called Lac des Deux-Montagnes and the scenery and the houses along it are delightful. Some of these houses are modern and very fine. Others are typical old-time French Canadian.

Near Senneville are **the ruins of an old fort**, built in 1692 as a protection against the Iroquois. It was near here, after the Lachine Massacre, that Greysolon Du Lhut and his band of *coureurs des bois* defeated the Iroquois at the Battle of the Lake of Two Mountains and saved the Island of Montreal from the fate of Lachine. **An historic monument** marks the spot. Du Lhut's own house was on the Place d'Armes in Montreal, but with his adventurous life as explorer, fur trader, fighter and leader of the *coureurs des bois* he could not have spent much time at home.

Between Senneville and Ste-Geneviève, you will find several **picnic grounds and parks** beside the water, the largest being Cap-St-Jacques Beach on the Lac des Deux-Montagnes. Opposite the village of Ste-Geneviève you will see Ile Bizard, connected by bridge with Montreal Island. The water which divides the two is the Rivière-des-Prairies. The road now passes through open farming country and, although it is still Highway 37, it is dignified with the name of Gouin Boulevard.

There is a bridge to Ile Jésus, the island which forms the opposite shore of the river. The Marlborough Golf and Country Club is here, and nearby there is a summer playground called the Belmont **Amusement Park**.

We followed the river down stream, past the Sault-au-Récollet to another bridge. A third bridge connects St-Vincent-de-Paul with Montréal-Nord. Across the water, we saw the sombre penitentiary walls rising high, with a cold forbidding greyness that subdued even the beauty of the river.

Montréal-Nord (Population 7,000). Although it is a separate town with a life of its own, as we drove by it seemed to us that it was merely an extension, or overflow, of the large city whose name it shares. This is true, to some extent, of every place on the island. To most visitors it is all Montreal, and the dividing lines, whether they be municipal, political or linguistic, are of little or no importance.

Bout-de-L'Ile, as its name implies, is at the foot of the island. At this point the Rivière-des-Prairies joins Rivière-des-Mille-Iles coming down from the north side of Ile Jésus, and both flow together into the St. Lawrence, or shall we say the Fleuve St-Laurent?

And now that we are at the end of it, perhaps we should tell you that the island is thirty miles long and ten miles across at its widest point. The shortest way back to the centre of town is to take Highway 2, which is Sherbrooke Street. Highway 37 will bring you back to the city on Notre Dame Street. This route follows the St. Lawrence River, goes through Pointe-aux-Trembles and covers the same area you saw from the sight-seeing boat, if you took the harbour cruise.

Another **variation on the homeward route** is to cross the Jacques Cartier Bridge to the south shore, follow Route 3 to the **Indian Village** of Caughnawaga, and return to Montreal via the Mercier Bridge. Local sightseeing companies call it the Indian Reservation Tour. This makes a loop trip of about twenty-five miles, and there are many points of interest along the way.

Half way across the Jacques Cartier Bridge, is Ile Ste-Hélène, so named by Champlain when he used the Place Royale as a fur trading post, in 1611. "In the middle of the river," he wrote, "there is an island about three-quarters of a league in circumference, where a good and strong town could be built, and I named it Ile de Ste-Hélène." The town did not materialize, and the island remained almost free of buildings, with the exception of an old fortification. St. Helen's Island is now **a public park**, **with large picnic areas**, and from it there is a fine view of the harbour, the bridges and the mountain.

Longueuil (Population 7,500). One of the most famous seigneuries of the French regime was that of Charles Le Moyne, Baron de Longueuil. It impressed even the Governor, for in describing it Count Frontenac said: "His fort and his house remind us of the fortified châteaux of France."

The fort was built of stone, flanked by four towers, and it stood on the south shore of the river, opposite Montreal, where the town of Longueuil now stands.

We had always been interested in the Dieppe innkeeper's son, Charles Le Moyne, who, as a lad of seventeen, had joined Maisonneuve's colony at Ville-Marie. The history of North America is filled with the amazing exploits of his eleven sons—Bienville, d'Iberville, Sainte Hélène, the two Châteauguays, and all the others including his namesake, Charles Le Moyne, Baron de Longueuil.

If you have read *High Towers*, by the famous Canadian-born novelist Thomas Costain, you will probably be anxious to see Le Moyne Seigneurie, and you will hurry across the bridge to Longueuil. But you will be disappointed, as we were. Practically nothing remains.

We found a plaque on the church, at the corner of St. Charles Street and the Chemin Chambly. It was inscribed in French, and it informed us that the church stood on the site of the stone fort built in 1685 by Charles Le Moyne.

Across the street there is **a stone house**, said to be **the oldest building still standing** in Longueuil. It may have belonged to the seigneurie. If so, it is about all that remains of the town's historic past.

We turned south and followed Route 3 for a short distance along the river.

St-Lambert (Population 7,000). Victoria Bridge, built almost a hundred years ago, connects this pleasant residential suburb with the city of Montreal.

Laprairie (Population 3,500) is the site of an early Jesuit Mission and of an old fort which saw much fighting between the French and English and the Indians in the unsettled days of the seventeenth century. In 1837 Laprairie became the northern terminus of the first railroad to be built in Canada. Today the town is industrial and the junction point of many highways.

If you continue along Highway 3, now called Laprairie Road, you will pass through Ste-Catherine, at the foot of the Lachine Rapids. It was near here that the little Mohawk Indian girl, Kateri Tekakwitha, came to live in

1676 to escape persecution because she had become a Christian. She is described as "the loveliest flower that blossomed among the Indians". Legends of the purity of her life have come down to us, and her tomb is visited by thousands of people each year. If you saw the Musée Historique Canadien in Montreal, you will remember the charming wax-works tableau of Kateri, kneeling before the altar she had built.

Caughnawaga (Population 3,000). The principal village on the **Iroquois Indian Reserve** is about five miles above the rapids. It was settled in 1716 by the Indians from Laprairie, who were sometimes called "the praying Indians" because they had been converted to the Christian faith. Their forebears were the warlike Iroquois, the bitter enemies of the French in the early days of New France, and the terror of every white settler in the colony.

There are about three thousand descendants of the Iroquois living in the village. Wearing their tribal dress, Chief Poking Fire and the others put on quite a show for visitors during the tourist season. The women of the village make and sell baskets and souvenirs.

Kanawaki Golf Club, with a large Montreal membership, is nearby.

Highway 3 goes to **Châteauguay** where there is a **Motel**, and continues on to Beauharnois and Valleyfield.

Beauharnois (Population 4,000). Nearby is the hydro-electric development of the Beauharnois Light Heat and Power Company, a huge power plant which diverts water from Lake St. Francis through a canal to Lake St. Louis, utilizing the fall of the Coteau, Cedar and Cascades Rapids of the St. Lawrence River.

Valleyfield (Population 18,000). This important industrial centre has one of Canada's largest cotton mills. The massive stone factories are unusual, giving the place a dramatic, almost medieval appearance. The city is nicely laid out around St. Francis Bay, where an **annual motorboat regatta** is held.

If you have done enough sight-seeing for today, the Honoré Mercier Bridge will take you from Caughnawaga back to Montreal.

There is one more thing which we think you should see before we leave Montreal behind us and go north into the Laurentian Mountains. Drive out Sherbrooke Street to Fort Street, a few blocks west of the Art Gallery and the Ritz-Carlton Hotel. In the garden of the Grand Seminary of the College of Montreal there are two old stone towers, which belong to the days when Montreal was Ville-Marie. They were built, in 1694, by the Gentlemen of St-Sulpice as part of a fortification to protect the town. Originally there were four towers with a great wall between them. They are called the Fort des Messieurs and, with the Seminary of St-Sulpice of which they are really a part, they are probably **the oldest buildings still standing in Montreal**.

And now let us leave history behind us for a while, and if you can tear yourself away from Montreal's good hotels, restaurants and shops, let us pack up and be on our way. La Province de Québec is enormous, and we have only covered one small corner of it.

Part Two

RESORTS AND RESOURCES IN NORTHERN QUEBEC

Chapter 4
THE LAURENTIANS

```
           ROAD LOG FOR HIGHWAY 11
        FROM MONTREAL TO MONT-LAURIER
  Miles
    0   Montreal
   15   Ste-Rose - Ile Jésus
   30   St-Jérôme
   38   Shawbridge
   42   Piedmont & St-Sauveur
   48   Ste-Adèle (Take road on right for
           Ste-Marguerite)
   54   Val-Morin & Val-David
   60   Ste-Agathe-des-Monts (Go right on
           30 for St-Donat)
   73   St-Faustin
   78   St-Jovite (Road on right goes to
           Mont-Tremblant)
  152   Mont-Laurier
```

WE HAVE BEEN TRYING for years to decide which is the best season to visit the mountain resorts, and we have come to the conclusion that any season is a good season. It depends entirely on what you want to do when you get there. Most of the hotels are open all year, and it is always holiday time in the Laurentians.

Strictly speaking the Laurentian Mountains extend all across the Province of Quebec, but in local Montreal parlance **the Laurentians** means merely that area which begins around Shawbridge and extends north to Mont-Tremblant Park. Its main travel artery, which is kept open all winter, is Highway 11.

It was July when we were last there, and we were completely won over to the merits of the Laurentians for summer holidays. Previously we had shared a rather deep-rooted idea that this is a winter resort, which, indeed, it is. Nowhere in the province will you find better **skiing**. There are **ski tows on almost every hill**, chair lifts, cross-country trails, ski schools and shops. To make the picture complete, a wide range of accommodations varying from the humblest to the most luxurious is to be found all along this 100 mile ski route.

The other seasons have something to offer, too. The **trout fishing** is good in May and June.

The **golf**, limited to about five courses, is pleasant, although not of championship calibre. The **swimming** is delightful, and there are boats and canoes available on most of the lakes.

Many of the resorts offer accommodations and meals well above the average. Several are definitely in the luxury class. All share a setting of unusual beauty.

But suppose we take you there and let you see for yourselves. We left Montreal on Highway 11, drove across **Ile Jésus**, past farms and market gardens, where we saw fields of the famous Montreal melons, and we crossed over the picturesque Rivière-des-Mille-Iles at Ste-Rose. Both the Laval-sur-le-Lac and the Islesmere Golf and Country Clubs are on the western tip of Ile Jésus.

We continued north on Route 11, past Rosemere Golf Club, through Ste-Thérèse and several miles of flat country to the foot-hills of the mountains.

St-Jérôme (Population 14,000). When we were in this city about fifteen years ago, we stayed at the Lapointe Hotel, and liked it. Last year the hotel was being rebuilt. What it may be like now remains to be seen, but you will probably find either the new Lapointe or the Maurice Hotel quite adequate for an overnight stop.

Shawbridge is the beginning, or perhaps we should say the end, of the best skiing country. **The Maple Leaf Trail**, laid out about fourteen years ago, begins at Labelle, near Mont-Tremblant Park, and ends at Shawbridge. On its eighty mile route, this famous ski trail passes close to the best known Laurentian resorts. It is marked by maple leaves on a yellow ground.

The hills around Shawbridge have an elevation of about 1,100 feet above sea level, and because of their proximity to Montreal, they are usually crowded with skiers on every winter week-end. If you want a quiet time, take our advice and come in the middle of the week, or else plan to go some distance away from the highway and the railroad station.

Four miles from Shawbridge, off the main highway on Echo Lake, there is **a delightful new all-year resort** called Country House—Old Hill. We think you will enjoy its club-like atmosphere and quiet comfort, either summer or winter. The rates are not too high.

During the summer there is **an information bureau** beside the highway near Shawbridge.

As we drove along, admiring the mountain scenery all around us, we had that carefree feeling of complete enjoyment, as if it really did not matter where we stayed in such a beautiful setting. However, as there are **more than two hundred inns, hotels, pensions, lodges and**

auberges listed in the Laurentian area, and as one can not stay at all of them, it is necessary to make a choice.

St-Sauveur, about four miles north of Shawbridge, is the centre of one of the most **popular skiing areas**. Five leading ski clubs have their headquarters here. The famous **Hill 70** is just south of the village, with downhill and slalom lay-outs. For the downhill runners there are rope tows on almost every hill, and a T-bar Alpine Ski Lift between Hills 70 and 71.

The village is a short distance off Highway 11, but do not overlook it because of that. It is charming. The main street is lined with small boarding houses, pubs, and restaurants. It caters to tourists, summer and winter, in a friendly and unpretentious way. St-Sauveur is a young resort, and unlike some of the luxury resorts farther north, its prices are scaled down to suit the youngsters who love to ski but who have to watch expenses.

At the foot of Hill 70 is Nymark's Lodge, the largest hotel in this area, a big log and stone building with **every facility for skiing**. On week-ends there are **dances, with a band**. For the summer season, there is a **swimming pool**, and the new 9 hole course of the St-Sauveur Golf Club starts and ends at the lodge.

Piedmont adjoins St-Sauveur to the north. There are many **private ski chalets** in this part of the mountains, and a number of small inns and lodges. Our favourite is the Mont-Gabriel Club, once called The Marquise. It was built as a private house, but it became a club fifteen years ago, and then a hotel.

You will find it atop a high hill, at an elevation of 1,300 feet, in its own 600 acre property. Its particular appeal for us is its club-like quality, and the complete

The Laurentians
(*Above*) Nowhere in the province will you find better skiing.
(*Below*) Club Mont Gabriel at Piedmont.

comfort of its artistically furnished rooms, each with its own open fireplace. The green grass growing on the unusual sod roof is charming, and so is the round swimming pool, one hundred and twenty feet in diameter. In the winter the pool becomes a skating rink.

The **ski school here is under the direction of the celebrated Hans Falkner**, who was knighted by King Albert I of Belgium for rescuing Professor Piccard from the Ober-Gurgl glacier in the Austrian Tyrol, where his stratosphere balloon had accidentally landed.

Mont Gabriel's T-bar Alpine Lift takes you to the very top of the mountain, from where there is a fine view of the villages of St-Sauveur and Piedmont in the valley below. **The Tamarack Trail is an exciting downhill run**, narrow and difficult, for expert skiers only. Scott's Slip is used by intermediates, and the Little Ober-Gurgl, named in honour of Hans Falkner, is fine for novices, and popular with everybody.

Mont Gabriel Club is **an all year resort**. We think it is one of the most pleasing small inns we have found anywhere. Luxury accommodations at luxury rates.

Back to the road again, and to the delights of motoring on a four-lane super highway, as we continue our tour of the Laurentians.

Another all-season holiday centre of considerable size and importance is the area around Ste-Adèle and Ste-Marguerite. There are several fine resorts in or near these villages, and a number of auberges and inns at moderate rates.

Ste-Adèle is divided in two. On the lower level, where Highway 11 runs through it, it is called Ste-Adèle-en-Bas. If you climb the hill to the west you will be in Ste-Adèle-en-Haut. This village has made a first rate effort

The Chantecler
Beyond you can see the village of Ste-Adèle.

to cater to the comfort and entertainment of visitors and it maintains **a Tourist Centre** at Ste-Adèle-en-Bas.

In the spring, from the middle of May until the end of June, the **fishing for speckled trout** is at its best, and the Laurentian Tours (Excursions Laurentiennes Enregistrées) will arrange everything for you. You can find them through the Tourist Centre, or through your hotel. They supply guides, canoes and camp equipment. The fishing licence, by the way, is only $5.25 a year for the whole family.

If you like, they will fly you in to some remote lake, seldom fished before. In July and August they will guarantee **a good catch of northern pike**. In the autumn, they will arrange your duck shooting or hunting trip.

Perhaps you are not a fisherman, and you may prefer to stay in one of the resort hotels.

You will find The Chantecler, situated at an elevation of 1,100 feet, just beyond the village on Lac Rond. The building is of early Norman architecture. All is smart, well-kept, up-to-date, and in good taste. We had a pleasant pine-panelled bedroom, overlooking the lake and tennis courts. Beyond we could see the village of Ste-Adèle, climbing up its mountain, on top of which there is a huge cross which is lighted at night. It shines out across the valley like a beacon at sea. In summer, the beach is delightful. Golfers can play either at Ste-Marguerite or at Val-Morin, both nearby. **Riding is popular**, too, and the trails which have been cut through the woods make good bridle paths. In the winter time, like all the Laurentian resorts, Chantecler stresses skiing, but if you do not care for that sport, you will certainly enjoy the **sleigh drives**, or the **dancing**, or the **sunbathing** on the sheltered terrace. The southern exposure makes it a fine place to sit in the sun, even on chilly days. You will enjoy the meals. We did. We have always liked The Chantecler, and although its rates are not low, we think they are in line with the quality it offers.

Another resort in the luxury class is the Ste-Adèle Lodge, at Ste-Adèle-en-Haut, one of the largest in the area. It has **a five hundred acre playground, with a swimming pool and tennis courts**. The front elevation of the Lodge on the main street of the village is not too impressive, but if you will go inside and walk through to the spacious grounds behind it, you will see what a pleasant place it is. In the winter, there is a ski shop and every facility to enjoy the slopes and hills of the village, as well as the miles of trails shared by all the hotels.

Both the Chantecler and the Ste-Adèle Lodge are very popular, in summer and winter, and it is a good idea to make reservations if you plan to stay at either one.

Before we leave Ste-Adèle, we must tell you about two small places which we think you will like. One is the Candle Inn, **a guest house of considerable charm**, a mile beyond the Ste-Adèle Lodge on the First Range Road. The other is the Quidi Vidi, **a restaurant**, not far from Highway 11 on the Ste-Marguerite road. It is built like a Normandy cottage, with parking space around it, and it specializes in **charcoal broiled steaks**. Open for lunch and dinner.

Ste-Marguerite is easily reached from Ste-Adèle by a good motor road, or by the Maple Leaf Trail, if it is winter and you prefer to ski there. On the way the trail passes one of the fastest and most difficult downhill runs. It is called Mt. Baldy, and unless you are in the expert class, or close to it, we do not advise you to try it. There are **many novice slopes nearby**, on the terrain which is used in the summer as a 9 hole golf course.

The Alpine Inn, another of the Laurentians' many all-year luxury hotels, is at Ste-Marguerite. It is a large and colourful log chalet, furnished in habitant style and kept in character throughout. It offers almost everything in the way of sports facilities for a happy holiday, summer or winter.

We liked the golf course, and we enjoyed swimming in the pool and in the North River, which flows through the hotel grounds. There are **tennis courts, a putting course and a riding stable** to round out the summer and autumn activities, and we doubt if you will ever see a lovelier sight than the Laurentian Mountains in late September, when the trees are turning from green to flaming red and gold.

In the winter there is skiing over well-maintained trails, on the popular Hill 60, and on Mt. Baldy. If you have come without your ski equipment, you may rent or buy what you need at the Alpine Inn's sport shop.

A few miles farther along the road, you will find **one of the oldest and still one of the nicest family resorts in the Laurentians**. It is called the Chalet Cochand, and it was begun almost forty years ago, by Emile Cochand and his wife, who came to Quebec from Switzerland. Their son, Louis, became a champion skier of the Laurentians. There is no place where you will find more enthusiasm for the sport, or better facilities for enjoying it, than at the Chalet Cochand. The touring trails on the property are kept in good condition, and the Chalet shares, with the other mountain resorts, a great network of cross-country trails and downhill runs.

This is an all year resort, and the summer season is

THE LAURENTIANS

(*Top*) The Alpine Inn, Ste-Marguerite. (*Middle*) Laurentide Inn, Ste-Agathe.
(*Bottom*) Chalet Cochand, Ste-Marguerite.

almost as popular as the winter. A unique feature of the Chalet Cochand is its planned amusements for the children. Games, picnics, beach and swimming activities are all arranged for the youngsters, and are carried out under the care of trained attendants, so that parents may relax and enjoy their holidays.

Private chalets may be rented by the season. The rates here are in the intermediate category, neither high nor low. It is just the sort of place a great many people are looking for, which makes reservations in advance a wise precaution.

Some distance along this same road, on Lac Masson, there is a modernistic resort which opened a few years ago with a burst of publicity—the Domaine d'Esterel. Its ultra-modern main building looks, to our conservative eyes, rather like a Hollywood movie set, and entirely out of keeping with its rustic background. The Esterel Lodge, built of logs, is quite pleasing, but it appears somewhat incongruous to us in its close proximity to the Blue Room and Esterel Theatre of modern American design, where movies and dancing supply the night life. The Domaine d'Esterel has a large following, and you might like it.

We have told you about our favourite resorts at Ste-Adèle and Ste-Marguerite, but as there are more than twenty hotels and inns from which to choose, we have not, by any means, exhausted the list.

Some people want the finest and most luxurious accommodations that money can buy, others want a small room with a private family where they can learn to speak French. A few prefer to rent a cottage or chalet and do their own housekeeping. The majority want comfortable rooms, in a pleasant resort at moderate rates. There are not many places in the world where one can truthfully say: "Here there is something for everyone." But it is true in the mountain resorts of the Laurentians.

If we have not come up with exactly the kind of place you are looking for, do not be discouraged. You will find it. It is here. As the villages are seldom more than five or six miles apart, you will not be too far from the centre of things, no matter where you may choose to stay. And that smooth, wide Highway 11 forms a connecting link, summer and winter.

Five or six miles north of Ste-Adèle, you will come to the next mountain resort area, usually referred to as Val-Morin, which includes the hills and valleys between Ste-Adèle to the south and Ste-Agathe on the north.

Val-Morin has **one of the best golf courses in the Laurentians**. It is a long and interesting nine holes, and twice around totals 6450 yards—a difficult par 72. The course is scenic and is well maintained. Although it is a private club, visitors are allowed certain privileges. Your hotel, or the Val-Morin Golf Club professional, will tell you when you may play.

The Far Hills Inn and Country Club on top of Mt. Gilbert is a comparatively new resort, two miles from the golf club. Highway 11 is kept open in all weather, but if the side roads should be blocked with snow, the Far Hills Inn will meet you in its private snowmobile.

At nearby **Val-David** mountain climbing is a feature. The village is built up with private cottages all along the river. Signs mark the Maple Leaf Trail and the ski tows.

Sixty miles from our starting point in Montreal, and still on Highway 11, we found ourselves at an elevation of 1,500 feet above sea level, in one of the long established all-year resorts.

Ste-Agathe-des-Monts (Population 6,000). There was a fashionable resort here when most of the other villages were nothing more than small farming centres. People came to Ste-Agathe from Montreal for a rest, for a change of air and altitude, and because it was "quaint". Some of the early resort hotels, once quite smart, have deteriorated through the years. Others have been well kept up. The place has become too crowded for our own complete enjoyment, but that, after all, is a matter of opinion.

Some of the hotels in this area make a special bid for New York patronage, and get it. Several places advertise "American Jewish Cuisine." Ste-Agathe is popular at all seasons, and its devotees come back, year after year. The Rue Principale has many shops, movie theatres, banks, restaurants, and the Mt-Sinaï Sanatorium.

Away from the crowded area, almost as if it wished to turn its back on the town, is the Laurentide Inn, beautifully situated on the shores of Lac des Sables. We found it quite delightful, with well arranged games and entertainment. The lake is large enough for sailing and for motor boats. The hotel has rowboats and canoes for its guests, and a sand beach. A concert pianist played effectively during the cocktail hour, and almost every evening there was a dance. One night there was a square dance, with old-time fiddlers.

We thought **the meals were well above average**, and the chiffon pies were something to dream about.

There are tennis courts at the hotel, and guests of the Laurentide Inn have playing privileges at the private Laurentian Golf and Country Club, where there is a nine hole course in a woodland setting.

As a winter resort, the Laurentide Inn can hold its

own with the best. It has a ski school, ski tows, and is
at the junction of a great many interesting trails, including the Maple Leaf.

There is a small inn on Lac des Sables that is very
popular with a group of selected guests. It is called
Craigie Manor, and it is run something like a club. It,
also, has playing privileges at the Laurentian Golf and
Country Club.

Among the hotels which feature American Jewish
cuisine are: Four Seasons Lodge, a small mountain-
lakeside resort; Manitou Lodge at Ivry, about four miles
north of town; the Vermont Hotel; and Sun Valley Lodge.

Ste-Agathe is the turn-off for Highway 30, a gravel
road which runs north to **St-Donat**, on Lac Archambault,
a popular fishing territory. Accommodations range from
small and inexpensive camps to the new Jasper-in-Quebec,
a modern resort. On the way this road passes Lac Brûlé,
where many Montreal families have their summer cottages and their winter chalets.

After leaving Ste-Agathe, we followed Highway 11 in
a northwesterly direction through a wooded, moun-
tainous country where there are long stretches of road
with few settlements of any kind. Some of the vistas are
wide and impressive.

At **St-Faustin** we turned off to see **the Provincial Fish
Hatchery**, about a mile from the highway. Only speckled
trout (*truite mouchetée*) are hatched here. There are a
number of round ponds in the garden, which contain
trout from six months to six years of age, ranging in size
from finger length to more than a foot. When the trout
are from six to eight months old, they are taken for an
aeroplane flight and are dropped from the air into the
many lakes through the Laurentians.

The hatchery is built of glacial boulders, and the grounds have been nicely landscaped.

Return to Highway 11, and a few miles farther on you will find yourself at the gateway to **that vast and wonderful area known as Mont-Tremblant Park**.

St-Jovite (Population 2,000). After passing the Norwood Golf Club, and a mountain stream with a waterfall, you enter the town of St-Jovite. On the main street you will find shops, churches, garages, and Le St-Jovite, a neat commercial hotel, with a dining room, which gets its share of skiers in the winter time. Well marked trails run through the town. The St-Jovite Theatre shows current release movies, usually in English but occasionally in French.

This is **the shopping centre and the gateway to a great number of resorts**. At the church in the middle of town you will see an amazing array of signposts pointing the way.

St-Jovite is the headquarters for Tom Wheeler's Airlines. He has planes to take you almost anywhere you might wish to go. He specializes in flying fishing parties in to the otherwise inaccessible lakes, and he can supply you with guides, canoes, and camping equipment. This method of trout fishing practically guarantees a large catch. The season for speckled, grey and brown trout is from the middle of April until the end of September, and we have seen many large and fine catches come out of the waters in the Mont-Tremblant area.

About three miles from town, on the Lac Tremblant road, you will come to one of the first **all-year holiday resorts** to be opened in the Laurentians. It is run by the Wheeler family, and at whatever season of the year you come, the Gray Rocks Inn has something to offer, including comfortable accommodations at moderate rates.

Fishing is featured for the spring and early summer; during July and August the **tennis** courts are in play; there are boats and canoes, and we found the **swimming** in Lac Ouimet just right. For the autumn they have a 9 hole golf course, trail riding and gorgeous scenery. When winter comes there is the famous **skiing** of the Mont-Tremblant slopes and trails. This is a pleasant, friendly resort, and if we have any criticism to offer it is merely that it is almost too popular, which tends to keep it crowded during the height of both the summer and winter seasons. We prefer it out of season, when it is not quite filled to capacity.

Mont-Tremblant. Beyond Gray Rocks Inn, about 8 miles from St-Jovite and 88 miles from Montreal, there is a village on Lac Tremblant. It is rather confusing that the village called Mont-Tremblant is on Lac Mercier and the railroad about three miles away from the mountain. The famous skiing resorts of the area are at Lac Tremblant which lies at the foot of the highest peak, and not at the railroad station.

We skirted the shore of Lac Ouimet, with islands nestling close to the water, and mountains rising high around it. In the village at Lac Tremblant, the Devil's River comes tumbling down in a picturesque waterfall. The long, deep lake stretches far into the distance, while over it towers Johannsen's Peak on Mont-Tremblant, 3,100 feet above sea level. This is the highest mountain in the Laurentians, and here you will find **the most spectacular skiing**. Johannsen's Peak was named after Herman Johannsen, who came to Canada fifty years ago from Telemark in Norway. His energy and enterprise were responsible for the building of the Maple Leaf Trail.

Here, in this northerly outpost of skiing, we were surprised to find some of the best and most luxurious accommodations in the Laurentians. One of the first hotels to be built here, just after the first Great War, was the Manoir Pinoteau, which is French Canadian in character and personnel. It has a delightful location in the village overlooking Lac Tremblant. It offers French cuisine, a variety of sports and amusements, and is one of the Laurentians' well-known luxury resorts at luxury rates.

On the outskirts of the village you will find the Tremblant Club. It is a new resort, run with loving care by its owner-manager. The bedrooms are attractively furnished, and each has a view across Lac Tremblant. The building is a log lodge, perched on the steep slope of a hill and surrounded by woods. There is no sense of crowding or of being hemmed in by houses. The Tremblant Club is rustic, north-country tranquility at its best. Guests may use the Bath and Tennis Club in the village, which has four *en-tout-cas* tennis courts, and the golf course at Gray Rocks Inn is only a few miles away.

The Bath and Tennis Club is at the entrance to the vast five thousand acre property of the Mont-Tremblant Lodge, probably **the best known and most unique resort in the Laurentians**. It was built about fifteen years ago by the late Joseph Ryan, grandson of Thomas Fortune Ryan. It is a perfect reproduction of a French Canadian habitant village, including a church. Guests are housed in the Lodge, the Inn, and in cottages, which are architectural gems, carefully furnished to carry out the French Canadian idea in every detail. Even the bed-spreads are handwoven in the province. It is a fabulous place, like something out of a fairy tale.

The summer season is pleasant with good swimming,

LAC TREMBLANT
(*Above*) Club Tremblant.   (*Below*) Mont-Tremblant Lodge.

boating and fishing, but its international fame rests firmly on the skiing facilities, as fine as any we have found in this country. There is a mile long aerial chair lift, which can carry five hundred skiers an hour up the mountain. There are T-bar lifts and rope tows and forty miles of trails and runs and slopes. Two of the favourite downhill runs in the expert class are the Kandahar and Ryan's Run. Three trails have recently been widened to 125 feet. They are: The Devil's Run, for experts; the Lowell Thomas, for intermediates; and the Sissy Shuss, for novices. Sissy Shuss! What a name!

An interesting building in this unusual "village" is the Chalet des Voyageurs, which is at the foot of the mountain, near the ticket office for the chair lift. This "Chalet" is part of the resort, but it is open to the travelling public, and visiting skiers are welcome to use its cafeteria and to dance to its orchestra.

You will hear lots of ski talk at Mont-Tremblant Lodge. If you wish to join a ski class, there are **ten instructors** to help you learn the fine points of the sport.

There is skiing on both sides of the mountain. For very cold weather, the southern slopes are best, but in late spring you will find snow on the northern slope long after it has disappeared in other places. The north side is well developed, with tows and lifts, and there you will find the comfortable Devil's River Lodge, an annex of Mont-Tremblant Lodge, which is less expensive and consequently very popular.

We think you will enjoy Mont-Tremblant Lodge even if you are not a skier. The lounges are spacious and comfortable, the Cowhide Bar and La Cabane popular gathering places, and La Boutique is as nice a little shop as you will find for woolens, handicraft, and sports clothes.

Perhaps it is hardly necessary to add that this is a

MONT-TREMBLANT

(*Above*) The mile long aerial chair lift.   (*Below*) Devil's River Lodge.

luxury resort and that the rates are not low; but they are no higher than the rates at other luxury resorts, and with forty miles of ski trails and a chair lift at your door, you really do get a good run for the money.

A new, wide gravel road, rough in places, leads back to Highway 11, via Mont-Tremblant Railway Station on Lac Mercier, and comes out at the northern end of the town of St-Jovite.

Labelle, about twenty miles up the road, is where the Maple Leaf Trail begins (or ends), and here we say good-by for the present to organized winter sports. Of course one can ski wherever there is snow but this is the end of the ski tows and lifts, and of the well-marked trails and runs.

We followed Highway 11 on its westward way for more than 50 miles, past lakes and mountains, through sparsely settled country, and we came at last to Mont-Laurier, on the wildly beautiful river called the Rivière-du-Lièvre.

Mont-Laurier (Population 3,000). There are garages here, and some small shops. It is something of a frontier town, an outpost settlement in the midst of forest and stream, which caters mostly to the lumberman and to the habitant and his family. Here you must make a decision. The direct route back to Montreal is over the road we have just taken, which is by far the best highway. Or you may continue on Highway 11, through the Gatineau Hills via Maniwaki to Wakefield, where there is a small inn, and on to Hull.

Another route, Highway 35, turns south at Mont-Laurier and follows the valley of the Rivière-du-Lièvre. This road will bring you to the Ottawa River about twenty miles down stream from Hull.

And lastly, there is the route on which we are about to embark. It covers hundreds of miles and is quite an expedition. It goes through the new La Vérendrye Park to the Abitibi gold mining area at the far northwestern end of La Province de Québec, almost three hundred miles away.

It is for you to choose. Come with us to Val-d'Or (The Valley of Gold) or join us, later, at Hull, or back in Montreal.

Chapter 5

LA VÉRENDRYE PARK AND THE MINES

WE LEFT "OLD" QUEBEC and its history when we left Montreal. The area we have just come through in the Laurentians, with its fashionable resorts, is comparatively new, although a few places go back to the nineties.

Now we are plunging into pioneer country as we cross the Barrière into La Vérendrye Park, **a vast fishing reserve of four thousand five hundred square miles,** surrounded on all sides by uncounted lakes and innumerable rivers. The settlements you will encounter on your way north are too small to be called villages. There are a few scattered fishing camps, and here and there you

80

will see an isolated pioneer farm. The only route that leads through this great expanse of forest and stream is Highway 58, still a gravel road when we travelled it.

For a long time this area had no name. It was referred to, vaguely, as Mont-Laurier-Senneterre, because the road through it runs between those towns. Now the Government of the Province of Quebec has given it an official title, La Vérendrye Park. It was named in honour of the famous explorers, Pierre Gaultier de Varennes, Sieur de la Vérendrye and his sons, who, in 1742, explored the vast territories of the American north-west and discovered the Rocky Mountains.

La Vérendrye was born in Trois-Rivières, in 1685, the son of the governor of that place. Three Rivers was one of the most important towns in the early French Colonial days, and we will go there, later, to visit the site of La Vérendrye's birthplace; but now something of his pioneer and adventurous spirit must be with you as we travel northward through the fishing reserve which bears his name.

This is **a trip for keen fishermen. Speckled trout, grey trout, doré (yellow pickerel), and northern pike are plentiful**. Guides are available, with boats and complete camping equipment. We think **the most satisfactory place to stay** is O'Connell Lodge, on Lac des Loups. It is a well established camp and a popular one.

Like all the Provincial Parks, La Vérendrye is **a game reserve**, and no hunting is permitted, but trips with guides can be arranged at O'Connell Lodge to hunt for moose and deer in nearby territory, outside the reserve.

If you are not planning to stay over in the park, but are merely driving through to the mining country, you will be glad to know that the Lodge has a special **dining room for transients**, and if it is lunch or dinner time, we suggest that you stop here for a meal. It is almost a hundred miles to the nearest village.

About 18 miles beyond the O'Connell Lodge, on the shore of Lac Rapide Bay, the Department of Game and Fisheries of Quebec has built **a number of small fishing camps**. The cottages will accommodate from two to four people, and are completely furnished with linen, dishes, and everything else you are likely to need, including fishing boats and canoes, and a good supply of firewood. As Lac Rapide forms a part of the large Cabonga Lake, with its myriad bays and islands, many miles of fishing waters are at your door. The camps may be rented by the day or week, from the end of May until the close of the season, from the Inspector of Game and Fisheries at Lac Rapide.

The Quebec fishing licence is $5.25 for the season, but a special permit at a fee of one dollar per day extra is required to fish in La Vérendrye Park Fishing Reserve.

Near the northern Barrière of the park there is a small settlement with a hotel where you can get gasoline. It is called Dorval Camp.

You will probably be surprised, as we were, to find yourself crossing the Ottawa River on Highway 58. It is called here Rivière-Outaouais. It winds its devious way from the great reservoir of Cabonga Lake towards Témiscamingue, and by the time it reaches the cities of Ottawa and Hull it has almost completed a circle.

Shortly after you leave La Vérendrye Park you will be in **Quebec's spectacular mining area**. At the village of Louvicourt there is a choice of roads. Highway 58 goes north to Senneterre and the clay belt. Highway 59 goes west to Val-d'Or and the mines.

Senneterre (Population 1,500) is on the Canadian

National Railway, and it is a distributing centre for forest industries and fish. West of it lies the agricultural belt, reached by Highway 45.

Amos (Population 6,000). Fifty miles west of Senneterre, you will come to this progressive town, the largest and most important place in the farming area. It was named in 1914 in honour of the wife of the Premier of Quebec, Lady Gouin, whose maiden name was Amos. It has a number of shops, small commercial hotels, movie theatres and service stations.

If you have come north to see the gold fields, you should take Highway 59 when the roads fork at Louvicourt. Along this route you will find many of Quebec's most famous mines and smelters.

Val-d'Or (Population 5,000). The Valley of Gold! Perhaps the name is more beautiful than the town, but one does not come to a mining country looking for the unspoilt beauties of nature. Here begins the 100 mile Golden Chain, from Val-d'Or to the Ontario boundary line.

Less than two hours' drive westward, along Highway 59, you will come to the twin towns of Rouyn-Noranda, the hub of the gold and copper mining. On the way you pass through **the mining town of Malartic**. There is much of interest here if you wish to see the real natural resources of the country.

At most of these towns there are **small commercial hotels**, some of which can offer you rooms with private baths.

Rouyn-Noranda (Population 15,000). The name Noranda is a coined word, made from North and Canada. The town is on Lake Tremoy, one mile north of Rouyn, and as you enter it from any direction you will see the great chimneys of the immense smelters towering high above the surroundings.

The pioneer discovery of gold in Northwestern Quebec was made in 1906 at Lake Fortune. The mine was operating by 1911 as the Lake Fortune Mining Company, and was more or less responsible for the gold rush to this part of the country that year.

Among the prospectors who came to Quebec in those early days was Edmund H. Horne, the discoverer of Noranda. He came back three times, never quite finding what he was looking for, but playing a hunch that there was gold in the vicinity of Lake Tremoy. In 1920, as he was unable to finance further explorations, some of his friends in New Liskeard, Ontario, formed a syndicate to grubstake him. It was called the Tremoy Lake Syndicate, and with the money thus obtained, he staked the claim to the now famous Horne Mine at Noranda, one of the world's largest copper-gold-silver-pyrite producers.

In 1922 the Noranda Mines Limited was incorporated, and production was started in 1927, eighteen years after its discovery by Horne. The "Lucky Ten" who grub-staked him all made fortunes. In 1925 the original share-holders were given one hundred new shares for every share they held, and twelve years later these new shares were selling as high as $84.00 on the Toronto Stock Exchange.

Lake Fortune Mine was the beginning—a failure. Noranda is the spectacular climax, and a fitting one. Its story is one of the fabulous true fairy tales of the magical Valley of Gold.

Noranda-Rouyn is more than 400 miles away from the city of Montreal if you travel by the shortest route, which is the road through the Laurentians and La

Vérendrye Park. If you should drive by way of the Ottawa River Valley the distance is over 500 miles, and much of the trip must be made in the Province of Ontario, as there is no through road on the Quebec side of the river.

We are reasonably sure that very few of you will have come with us on this long journey to the mining country. We have included it here for the *voyageurs* of the modern age, those adventurous spirits who like to go far afield to see everything. Most of you will be content to enjoy the luxury of the Laurentian resorts, or the comparative comfort of the La Vérendrye Park fishing camps.

But now it is time for all of us to meet again, and to continue our journey together. Suppose we make a rendezvous for dinner at the famous Café Henry Burger in the city of Hull, which is just across the river from Ottawa, the Capital city of Canada.

Chapter 6

THE OTTAWA RIVER VALLEY

THE STORY OF THE OTTAWA RIVER is essentially the history of Canada from 1613, when Champlain first explored it, to the present time. Today it is the site of the nation's capital, which bears its name. Three hundred years ago it was the great fur trading route, and was the highway by which La Vérendrye, Radisson, Du Lhut, and other early French explorers travelled westward in their quest for a route to China.

It was originally called the Rivière-des-Algonquins. The word Ottawa is derived from the name of the Indians, a tribe of the Algonquin family, who lived on

THE OTTAWA RIVER VALLEY
Lumbering near Hull.

Manitoulin Island and who used the Ottawa as their trade route when they brought their furs to market on the island of Montreal.

The English spelling of the name is Ottawa, but the French still use the older form of Rivière-Outaouais. This is a turbulent river throughout most of its three hundred and eighty-five miles. A tribe of Indians who traced their descent from "The Great Beaver" believed the falls and cataracts of the river were the remains of dams built by their ancestors.

Long before the coming of the white man, this was a much used canoe route of the Huron and Algonquin Indians. It was a long and tedious paddle, with many portages but it avoided the country of the war-like Iroquois who lived along the upper St. Lawrence and around Lake Ontario.

When Champlain first paddled up the Ottawa, in May 1613, he went only as far as Allumettes Island, about one hundred miles upstream from the present city of Hull. He found a tribe of Algonquin Indians who, because of their strategic position in the middle of the river, could close the waterway to traffic, if they wished to do so. Other Indian tribes paid toll for the privilege of using their territory, in the form of yearly presents, as was the custom among Indians.

Champlain found them willing and anxious to trade, and the first great highway of commerce was opened to the west.

Hull (Population 40,000). A busy industrial city, dominated all along its river frontage by the huge mills of the E. B. Eddy Pulp and Paper Company, Hull suffers by comparison with the unusual beauty of the city of Ottawa on the opposite shore. One of the old portage routes around the Chaudière Falls came through Hull. It was traversed by explorers, missionaries, and fur traders on their way from the St. Lawrence River to the Great Lakes, and beyond, from Champlain's time until the middle of the nineteenth century.

The town itself was founded by Philemon Wright in 1800. It was named after Hull in England. Wright imported cattle from Great Britain, established an agricultural community, and conducted the first lumber raft on the Ottawa River from Hull to Montreal, in 1806. From that day lumbering began to supersede the fur trade in importance.

Viscount Alexander of Tunis, Governor-General of Canada, unveiled a statue of Philemon Wright in June, 1950, commemorating the one-hundred and fiftieth anniversary of the founding of Hull. The monument stands in a busy square, on Highway 8.

About three miles west on this highway, known as Aylmer Road, you will pass the Royal Ottawa Golf Club (private), next to which is the Glenlea Golf and Country Club, an 18 hole course, where out-of-town guests may play. Farther west on Aylmer Road is **the Connaught Park Jockey Club**, and a short distance beyond it is **the 18 hole golf course of the Gatineau Country Club**, where visitors are welcome.

North of Hull, in the Gatineau Hills, the Ottawa Ski Club has built lodges and laid out some interesting trails and runs. Visitors may join the club as out of town members.

A road goes north through the Gatineau Valley and connects with the Laurentian Highway at Mont-Laurier. Both roads are known as Highway 11, and together they form a loop tour of 275 miles through the mountains from Montreal to Hull.

We are not forgetting that we have a rendezvous with you at the Café Henry Burger. Most people refer to it as Mme. Burger's, and it looks so much like a private house that you can easily pass it if you are not watching for the number. It is at 69 Laurier Street, and Highway 8 passes the door. Madame Burger, who now owns and runs this "typically French" restaurant, is the widow of a Swiss, once chef at the old Waldorf-Astoria in New York and, later, maître d'hôtel of Ottawa's famous Château Laurier. The restaurant enjoys a fine reputation, and is open every day, including Sunday, for lunch and dinner.

The drive down the Ottawa Valley from Hull to Montreal is pleasantly picturesque, and we found it surprisingly free of heavy traffic.

We stopped near the bridge over the Gatineau to watch men working on a log boom. Logs were coming down the river in a seemingly endless stream, and here they were being sorted, checked, and sent on their way via different channels. Farther along, at the village of Gatineau, there was a log boom in the Ottawa, between the International Paper Company's mill and Kettle Island.

At the small pulp and paper town of Masson, the road from Mont-Laurier meets Highway 8, having followed the course of the Rivière-du-Lièvre for ninety-eight miles through the Gatineau Lake country.

From here down, the highway runs fairly close to the Ottawa River, through mixed farming country, to Papineauville and Montebello, names linked with that of the fiery orator and rebel, Louis-Joseph Papineau, leader of the Lower Canada Rebellion of 1837.

Montebello (Population 1,500). Farms border the river.

The Main street of the town follows the higher ground.
The Manor House of Montebello is here, home of the
Papineau family. It is in the private grounds of the
fashionable Seigniory Club, and as no one is admitted
except members and their guests, there is little chance
for a passing traveller to see this interesting old house.
The town itself, predominantly French-speaking, has the
usual stores and garages. Le Paysan Shop has woolens
and handicraft for sale.

At Point-au-Chêne and Calumet Falls there is some
interesting scenery—lumber booms, rivers, and a waterfall over a hundred feet high, which tumbles down from
the hills to join the Ottawa River.

Grenville is on the canal which was begun in 1819 to
overcome the treacherous rapids of the Long-Sault, the
great hindrance to easy navigation on the Ottawa for
over two hundred years. The Grenville Canal has five
locks, 200 feet long and 45 feet wide, with a depth of
water on the sills of 9 feet 6 inches. The village is an
important crossroads, for this is where Highway 8 goes
inland to take a short cut to Montreal, via the industrial
town of Lachute.

Although it is a little longer and narrower, we hope
you will follow Highway 29, **the historic river road**. It
would be a pity not to see the old squared timber houses
at Cushing, dating back to pioneer days, and the villages
of Carillon and St. Andrews East are much too interesting to miss.

Carillon. You will certainly want to stop here to see the
really worth-while **Museum of the Historical Society of
Argenteuil County**. It is housed in the old Carillon
Barracks, built in 1829 for the Royal Engineers who had
been sent from England to construct the canals.

The barracks stand between the river and the road, at the foot of the Long-Sault Rapids. From the verandah you can see the spot where Dollard des Ormeaux and his sixteen companions from Montreal made their heroic stand, in 1660, against the attack of seven hundred Iroquois warriors.

Of the museum exhibits, we thought the collection of native birds and their nests was particularly interesting. It even included a specimen of the extinct passenger pigeon. Another room has an unusual exhibit of ships models, depicting the history of navigation on the Ottawa River.

Carillon lies in part of the Seigneurie of Argenteuil, originally granted to Charles d'Ailleboust in 1682 by Count Frontenac, Governor of Canada. Also forming part of the old Seigneurie was the present village of St. Andrews East, just two miles from the Carillon Barracks.

St. Andrews East is sometimes called St-André on the maps, but the English name suits it much better. As we walked along its quiet, elm shaded streets, and beside its old mill stream, we felt as if we were back in Georgian days, during the Regency, for many of the buildings in St. Andrews East date from that time. The old mill was built in 1803, **the first paper mill in Canada**. It still stands, although considerably enlarged and altered, and the same river turns the wheel that saw the humble beginning of one of Canada's major industries.

The Anglican church, called Christ Church, is a simple and lovely red brick building which stands on the main street, opposite the Town Hall, and is authentic Georgian colonial architecture and not a reproduction. Its founder was the Rev. Joseph Abbott, M.A., whose eldest son was born in the parish in 1821, just two years

ST. ANDREWS EAST
Old mill built in 1803, the first paper mill in Canada.

after the church was built. This child grew up to become Sir John J. C. Abbott, Prime Minister of Canada.

Another old building is St. Andrew's Presbyterian Church, built of stone in 1818. There is a rugged sturdiness to the architecture, characteristic of the early Scottish settlers. The unusual red brick Roman Catholic Church near the bridge, although comparatively new, was well designed to fit into its mellow surroundings.

There are a few interesting houses, with old-fashioned gardens, that help to carry out the illusion that this is another world, or at least another age. Even the St. Andrews Golf Club merely reminds us that golf is a "Royal and Ancient" game.

One of the loveliest things about Quebec is the charm of its villages. They are so varied, so unusual, so unexpected. No matter how small it is, each seems to have an individuality of its own. It may be the great church around which the tiny village clusters; it may be the quaint Norman-French architecture of its houses; or perhaps it is the curious, high and twisted outdoor stairways that catch and hold your attention. Whatever it may be, a Quebec village is never dull nor uninspired. Even in a province with so many charming villages, St. Andrews East remains in our memory as a very special place.

Across the Ottawa River from St. Andrews East, beyond the islands, you may be able to see **Rigaud**, Quebec. The Ontario boundary line dashed off at a tangent from the river at the Carillon dam. **The Shrine of Our Lady of Lourdes** is at Rigaud, where an Oratory and Grotto dedicated to the Virgin have become a place of pilgrimage.

Sixteen miles down the river from St. Andrews East, the Ottawa widens into the Lake of the Two Mountains.

(*Above*) Trappist Monastery, Oka, Where the Cheese Comes From
(*Below*) Canal at Grenville, Begun in 1819 to Overcome the
Treacherous Rapids of the Long Sault

One of these mountains is **Oka, where the cheese comes from**.

Oka (Population 1,500). At one time there was an Indian village on this site, and for many years it was an important Indian gathering place, for this is the meeting of many waters—the Ottawa, the Rivière-des-Mille-Iles, and the Rivière-des-Prairies, and beyond Ile Perrot are Lac St-Louis and the St. Lawrence.

Fishing for pike and maskinonge is popular in the Lac des Deux-Montagnes. Four miles east of Oka, on Highway 29, you will come to **the Trappist Monastery**, called Abbaye de Notre-Dame-du-Lac, La Trappe d'Oka. It is in a really beautiful setting of mountain and farmland. Here the famous Oka cheese is made. Visitors are admitted through the main gate to the garden, and to some of the buildings.

And now we leave the valley of the Ottawa, for here the river joins itself with the other tributaries of the St. Lawrence. Follow Highway 29 and it will bring you to another of Quebec's pleasant villages.

St-Eustache (Population 2,000). French Canadian in every way, St-Eustache has unusual beauty in the Rivière-des-Mille-Iles with its many islands, and in the smaller Rivière du Chêne which flows through the centre of the town.

The handsome Roman Catholic church on the main street dominates the scene. It was the site of the battle of St-Eustache in 1837, one of the tragic episodes in the Papineau Rebellion. The rebels used the church as a last defence, rather than surrender when the government troops moved in, and in the ensuing fight not only the church but the whole village was burned and many lives were lost.

In the meantime, Papineau had fled to the United States. He returned, ten years later, to sit again in Parliament. A brilliant and inflamatory orator, he had stirred up more trouble than he had intended, and he maintained to his dying day that he had never advocated armed rebellion.

And now, if the day is drawing to a close, perhaps you would like to bunk down for the night. The Bellevue Hotel, opposite the church, is **a small village inn** which offers comfortable accommodations. If you want something smarter or grander, Montreal with its many fine hotels is only twenty miles away.

Part Three

STRONGHOLD OF THE FRENCH REGIME

Chapter 7

THE ST. LAWRENCE RIVER FROM MONTREAL TO QUEBEC

ROAD LOG FOR HIGHWAY 2
From Montreal to Quebec

Miles

Miles	
0	Montreal
15	Bout-de-l'Ile Bridge
19	Repentigny
40	Lanoraie
48	Berthier - Lac St-Pierre. Ferry to Sorel
67	Louiseville
73	Yamachiche
87	Trois-Rivières - St. Maurice River. Ferry
90	Cap-de-la-Madeleine. Route 19 goes to Shawinigan Falls and Grand'mère
139	Donnacona
166	Quebec

An alternative route is Highway 3 along the south side of the river, from Longueuil to Levis, 186 miles.

We left Montreal Island on Highway 2 and followed the St. Lawrence River down stream. From the Ontario border until it reaches the sea, this mighty river flows entirely through the Province of Quebec. It can be paralleled fairly closely all the way on a good paved road.

The St. Lawrence River—Canada's Highway of History! For over four hundred years it has been a vital route for travel and trade. It drains all the Great Lakes. The Ottawa River, the Richelieu, the St. Maurice, the Saguenay, and a hundred or more smaller rivers and streams are its tributaries. The four largest cities of the province are along its shores, and so are the oldest villages, and the most fashionable resorts.

Repentigny. Like most of the towns and villages you will pass through on your way to Quebec, Repentigny is steeped in the history of ancient Indian wars and the struggle of the early French settlers to survive. There was a fort here, in 1691, which figured in a fierce battle against the Iroquois. During this fight young François de Bienville, one of the eleven sons of Charles Le Moyne, was shot and killed. After the death of François, one of his brothers took the name and became Le Moyne de Bienville, the founder of New Orleans.

A number of overnight cabins and summer cottages have been built recently in the vicinity of Repentigny, but a few of its old landmarks still stand.

The river is flat and marshy in places, and the road runs so close to the water that you can watch the steamships passing.

For many miles the highway is like a long street through a pretty village, reminiscent of the quaint paintings of old Quebec one sees on Christmas cards. On one side of the road is the St. Lawrence River, on the other tree-shaded cottages and Normandy farm houses. Here and there you will find a "Plage"—or small summer resort—with cabins and guest houses, neat and well painted, strung along the beach.

Lavaltrie. As we passed through the village, with its characteristic Lombardy poplar trees, we were amused to see a large sign which said: "English Spoken". It gave us the odd feeling of being abroad, in our own country. We soon found, however, that there was a good reason for the sign. In many of these small resort villages English is *not* spoken, as they cater almost entirely to the local French Canadians. There were moments when we felt that we were motoring through France. The poplar trees, the old-world stone cottages and churches, and the signs all in French strengthened the illusion.

Lanoraie (Population 1,000) is another of the typically French Canadian summer resorts. There are a number of private cottages, gaily painted in charming combinations of red, blue and white, and some in yellow and orange. In summer the whole place radiates a happy holiday mood, with its flags flying and its cheerful colour schemes.

A few miles farther on you will pass a **Provincial Forest Station**. Near here the river narrows, and on the opposite shore you can see the city of Sorel. When the river widens again it is known as Lac St-Pierre.

To anyone who has read Drummond's famous French-Canadian poems, Lac St-Pierre will be remembered as the place where the wood scow, *Julie Plante*, "bus' up". Whenever we have been there, the water has been calm and tranquil, but it is a large lake and we can well believe that there are many days when "the wind she blow, blow, blow", as described so picturesquely in *The Wreck of the Julie Plante*.

Berthier (Population 3,000) is also called Berthier-en-haut, and sometimes Berthierville, to distinguish it from the village of the same name farther down the river.

Both places were named in honour of Captain Alexander Berthier, who was given the land as a seigneurie in 1673.

If you want to see Lac St-Pierre, keep to the right as you drive into town. There is a place to park at the boat landing, in front of Berthier's leading commercial hotel. This is a busy town, serving a farming area, and you will find the usual shops and garages are on the main street, one block in from the lake.

Berthier was the home of James Cuthbert, who fought against the French at Louisburg and at Quebec, and became aide-de-camp to General Murray. After the battle of the Plains of Abraham, which marked the end of the French regime in Canada, Cuthbert was chosen to go to England with the news that Quebec had fallen. In 1765, after he returned to Canada, he acquired the seigneurie of Berthier. You can still see the old Protestant church, now in ruins, built on the Cuthbert property, and reputed to be the first Protestant church erected in the Province.

Between Berthier and Louiseville the highway is straight and fast, and runs inland out of sight of lake and river.

Louiseville (Population 4,000). As Quebec goes, this is a new town. Founded in 1714, it was incorporated in 1879 and named for Princess Louise, wife of the Marquis of Lorne who was then Governor-General of Canada.

We like the Château Louise, a small town commercial hotel of the better type. Outside it has a pleasant old-fashioned look, with Victorian verandahs and flower boxes planted with double petunias. Inside it has been modernized. Many of the bedrooms have private baths, and if the dining room is closed, you can have a snack in the cocktail bar and coffee shop.

Its name and the outward appearance of the hotel are

the only Victorian things about Louiseville. It is predominantly French-speaking, and many of the houses have the long outside stairways so characteristic of French Canadian towns. We counted at least ten varieties, all the way from a perilously steep and straight flight to one that was a perfect two-story spiral.

You will find, in this part of Quebec, that all the radios are tuned to French-speaking stations, and that no one bothers to translate any of the signs and notices into English.

After Louiseville we ran through **Yamachiche**, a centre for dairying and market gardening. The country was flat. The road looked like a wide grey ribbon stretched across a billiard table. The towers of the Canadian Marconi Company rose high above a group of thatch roofed barns.

The seigneurie here was granted to Pierre Boucher. His career is somewhat reminiscent of that of Charles Le Moyne, and was typical of those adventurous days. As a boy of thirteen he came to Canada from France. After spending four years living with the Huron Indians to learn their language and their ways, he became interpreter for the French garrison at Quebec. When he was twenty-three years old he moved to Trois-Rivières, a thriving young fur trading post which had been founded a few years earlier under Champlain's orders. Later Boucher became the governor of Trois-Rivières, and was also given the seigneurie of Boucherville, near Longueuil.

About five miles west of Three Rivers there is a Motel beside the St. Lawrence. It is called the Château Bleu, and it has several large cottages and a lunch room. If you like motels, you will find this one a convenient overnight stop.

Trois-Rivières (Population 50,000). Many people driving through Three Rivers for the first time are in such a hurry to get to Quebec that they scarcely stop to look at Canada's second oldest city. They think of it as just another busy manufacturing centre given over to the pulp and paper industry.

That was our first impression, too, because this is **one of the most important paper manufacturing cities** in the world. But it is more than that. Trois-Rivières goes back over three hundred years, and we urge you to pause long enough to see its ancient buildings and to delve a bit into its history. You will find it rewarding.

Three Rivers was founded in the year 1634, eight years earlier than Montreal. Monsieur de La Violette (commonly called Laviolette) had been sent from Quebec by Champlain to build a fur trading post and fort at the mouth of the St. Maurice River. La Violette and a company of artisans landed at a spot near the present handsome Post Office and began building the Fort de Trois-Rivières. Turcotte Esplanade, overlooking the waterfront, is built on the foundations of the old fortifications. Immediately adjoining the Esplanade, along Notre-Dame and the Rue des Ursulines, you will find what remains of the old city, buildings that go back to the very beginnings of Canada.

Father Le Jeune, who came to this new settlement close on the heels of La Violette, wrote that the French named this place Trois-Rivières because here a beautiful river enters the St. Lawrence by three main channels.

Your first call, before you go exploring, should be at the **Chamber of Commerce** and **Tourist Bureau**, at 166 Rue Bonaventure, half a block from the Post Office. The Tourist Bureau is housed in the interesting and historic old Boucher de Niverville Manor house, built about 1740,

(*Top*) MONASTERY AND CONVENT OF THE URSULINES AT TROIS RIVIÈRES
(*Middle*) LOUISEVILLE (*Bottom*) JACQUES CARTIER BRIDGE AT MONTREAL

and occupied by Joseph-Claude Boucher de Niverville, soldier and explorer, during the twenty years that he was superintendent of Indians in the district of Trois-Rivières. The old house is a fine example of French colonial architecture. The Tourist Bureau will give you a warm welcome, and will supply you with a map of the city and any information you may require.

Our suggestion is that you park your car and walk through the old part of town. It is a small area. Only a few of the ancient houses remain, but this was the "Cradle of Explorers". It bred men like La Vérendrye and his sons, discoverers of the Rocky Mountains. It was the home of Radisson and Groseilliers, whose explorations and ingenuity were responsible for the formation of the now famous Company of Adventurers of England Trading into Hudson's Bay. To get a true picture of what life was like in seventeenth century North America, one must visit Trois-Rivières as well as Quebec.

If you walk east from the Post Office, along Rue Notre-Dame, you will pass the **Place d'Armes**, a tiny park which has been in existence since 1650. Opposite it, much altered and enlarged, is one of **the oldest buildings** still standing in the city—the Godefroy de Tonnancourt house, built around 1680. Farther along the same street at the corner of Rue St-François-Xavier you will come to the mellow old church that dates back to 1699. The building was originally a convent of the Récollet Friars, the first religious order to settle in La Nouvelle-France. It was rebuilt in 1754 and became St. James Anglican Church after the conquest of Quebec.

This must have been the fashionable residential district, because immediately across the street, at 834 Rue des Ursulines, is the house built in 1756 by Major de Gannes, and lived in at a later date by Judge Vallières de

TROIS RIVIÈRES
The Tourist Bureau is housed in the historic Boucher de Niverville Manor house,
built about 1740.

Saint-Réal. Next door, at number 802, is a charming, ivy-mantled stone cottage. An historic marker in the garden reads in translation:

> HERE LIVED MICHEL GODEFROY DE LINCTOT,
> FIRST WHITE CHILD BORN IN THE LAND OF
> THE THREE RIVERS THE 21ST OCTOBER, 1637

Every stone in this small corner of the city seems to pulsate with the life of a bygone age. Most impressive and noteworthy of the buildings is the Monastery and Convent of the Ursulines. Just beyond the old houses, you will see its steep pitched roof with a sun dial set in the gable. The Ursulines came to Trois-Rivières in 1697, and began building the convent and hospital three years later. General Montgomery's wounded soldiers were cared for here in 1776. About fifty years ago the buildings were restored and substantial additions made.

If you will walk back to Turcotte Esplanade, immediately behind the old Anglican church, you will come to the site of the house where La Vérendrye was born, in 1685.

Beneath the shade of giant elm trees, overlooking the St. Lawrence River, **a memorial** has been erected to the memory of the many famous explorers who lived in Trois-Rivières. One of these was Jean Nicolet, the young interpreter and adventurer, who took with him a robe of Chinese damask embroidered in birds when he went west in search of a route to China so that he would be suitably dressed when he arrived at the court of Cathay.

The names of Radisson and his brother-in-law, Groseilliers, of the Hudson's Bay Company, are also carved on the memorial, and there are many others. There is a special monument to the La Vérendrye family, the most illustrious of all the sons of Trois-Rivières.

"*Gloire et hommages*" is cut in the stone, and everyone who has read stories of the voyages of discovery of the early French Canadian explorers will agree that "Glory and homage" is the least we can offer them for their great courage and tenacity of purpose in opening up for mankind a whole new world.

If you have not yet had your fill of history, drive out Rue des Forges, past the battle field of the Revolutionary War of 1776, to **the Exhibition Grounds with its large outdoor swimming pool**. Continue on Boulevard des Forges for about 9 miles to **the ruins of the old foundry**, built in 1738 and conceded to be the first iron industry established in Canada.

Perhaps you have done enough sight-seeing and would like to find a hotel where you can settle for a night or two while you explore the St. Maurice River Valley and the surrounding country.

We all have our own ideas about the kind of hotels we like. Few places appeal to everyone. This is a stop for those who prefer urban communities to the wilds, and for those who are looking for the unusual.

The Château de Blois, on Highway 2 at 225 Laviolette Boulevard, has steadfastly maintained its old world appearance and each time we go there we feel that we have stepped into **a French inn** not too far from Paris. The north-east wing of the hotel was built in 1828, and was the residence of the first mayor of Three Rivers. Most of the furnishings are French antiques. We have always been pleased with the meals in the *grande salle à manger*, which is open from 7 a.m. until midnight. Rates are no higher than those at most small commercial hotels.

Mrs. Franklin D. Roosevelt stayed at the Château de Blois in 1949 and describes it in her book, *This I Remember*, as a place which "has the atmosphere of a hotel in some little provincial town in France."

One of the most popular restaurants in Three Rivers is a kind of bakery-tea-room, or *pâtisserie,* called Kerhulu's, at 1354 Notre-Dame Street. Although a branch of the famous Quebec restaurant of the same name, this one is smaller and the menus are less inspired.

There is **a golf course** on the island of St-Christophe, and **a canoe club** named after Radisson on the St. Maurice River.

A disaster befell Trois-Rivières on a 26 below zero night in 1951, when the $5,000,000 Duplessis Bridge over the St. Maurice River collapsed. Four spans of the 2,000 foot steel and concrete two year old bridge crumbled and fell. The sound described by an eye-witness was "like the roar of an earthquake". The cause of the disaster was variously given as sub-zero weather, faulty construction, and sabotage. Traffic had to detour by way of Shawinigan Falls, up the St. Maurice River Valley, until ferries could be put into operation and a Bailey bridge erected.

The St. Maurice River Valley. Although the detour is no longer necessary, it makes an interesting drive, especially for anyone who wants to study Quebec's major industry, pulp and paper.

The St. Maurice River has been highly industrialized during the past few years, with the building of **giant hydro-electric power plants** capable of generating one million five hundred thousand horse power, but the valley has not sacrificed its beauty.

Highway 19, which runs north from Cap-de-la-Madeleine, is known as the Voyageurs' Trail. It is paved for the first thirty miles or so, and continues as a gravel road for another seventy miles into the wild north country beyond La Tuque.

It is not necessary to go far, however, to see and appreciate the St. Maurice River. The drive to Sha-winigan Falls and Grand'mère and back to Trois-Rivières can be done in about two hours and will give you a good idea of what the country is like.

Cap-de-la-Madeleine (Population 10,000). This town, situated on a cape overlooking both the St. Lawrence and the St. Maurice Rivers, has **a National Shrine** which is visited annually by hundreds of thousands of pilgrims and sight-seers. A wooden chapel was constructed in this place in 1659. The present stone chapel, built in 1714, houses the miraculous statue of Our Lady of the Cape, Queen of the Holy Rosary. The eyes of this statue became animated in 1888. With the approval of Pope Pius X, Notre-Dame du très Saint-Rosaire was crowned "Our Lady of Canada", in 1904, and five years later the Sanctuary was proclaimed a National Place of Pil-grimage.

Shawinigan Falls (Population 35,000). A new and rapidly growing city, with **huge pulp and paper mills**, a chemical plant and other industries, this promises to become one of Quebec's most important industrial centres. Its leading hotel is the Cascade Inn, near the falls.

Grand'mère (Population 10,000). Although it is only thirty miles from Trois-Rivières, Grand'mère is like another world. It has a frontier quality. This is not a resort in the usual sense but there is **a pleasant, reason-ably priced hotel** there, named the Laurentide Inn, which is quiet and comfortable. Near it there is **a champion-ship golf course** which we enjoyed playing. The golf course, tennis courts and the club house are **open to visitors**.

The Laurentide Inn stays open all year. In the winter it offers skiing, skating and curling, and it is rather fun to rent a sleigh and drive over the snow-covered byways to the tune of jingling sleigh bells. As an alternative to staying in Trois-Rivières, you might enjoy spending the night at Grand'mère.

Returning to Highway 2 at Cap-de-la-Madeleine we shall now continue on our way east. Most of you are probably anxious to get on to Quebec, that romantic old fortified city on the rock which has the power to lure so many visitors within its walls, no matter what the season.

After you leave Cap-de-la-Madeleine you will notice **a great display of handicraft** all along the route. Scenic hooked rugs suitable for playrooms or nurseries, hand-knit woolen socks and hand-tufted bedspreads are the principal articles offered for sale in this region.

Champlain (Population 800) is too small and unpretentious a place to be named after the man who has been called "the greatest Canadian of all time", but it has a certain charm. If the weather is hot and you feel in the mood for a swim, there are a number of cabins on the beach which you may rent by the day, and there is a characteristic handicraft shop in the village.

A short drive through pretty farming country brings you to another French Canadian summer colony.

Batiscan (Population 1,500). Here, also, you will find a river beach and several cabins and cottages for rent to overnight guests. River boats come in to the wharf, and the lighthouses add a nice nautical touch to the scene.

The village is at the mouth of the Batiscan River which is usually crowded with logs and fish traps.

A few miles farther on, you come to another of the numerous Ste-Anne's.

Ste-Anne-de-la-Pérade (Population 2,000). That so many towns and villages in the same province should be called Ste-Anne is confusing. Ste-Anne-de-la-Pérade has taken to calling itself simply La Pérade. This quaint old-world village, strung along a winding and narrow street with an impressive church towering over all the other buildings, is our idea of a typical French Canadian small town. If you are looking for local atmosphere, you will find plenty of it here, in the place where Madeleine de Verchères lived after her marriage.

Les Grondines is a small rural settlement, about forty miles from the city of Quebec. Although it is wide enough, the St. Lawrence River is so shallow at this point that we wondered how ocean-going steamships could find a channel between the rocks, but the lighthouse range on shore and the signal post in the river evidently succeed in keeping vessels off the shoals.

Between here and Quebec there are some beautiful examples of French colonial farm houses, and several simple but appealing wayside shrines.

Deschambault, the next village, has some particularly fine examples of stone *habitant* houses. It is well worth slowing your pace to observe the well-balanced lines of these old buildings, with their steep-pitched roofs and graceful simplicity of architecture. The style has lately been revived with success at Mont-Tremblant Lodge, and for small modern homes in many towns and cities.

Portneuf (Population 1,000) is another historic village worth more than a fleeting glance. The highway by-passes the main street, but you need not do so, and we hope you will take the few minutes needed to drive through the centre of Portneuf, slowly, so that you may absorb its **unique local colour**. This village has changed little with the passing years and with a minimum of imagination you will be able to visualize life as it was lived here under the French regime.

After climbing the hill and passing through another charming old village, called **Cap-Santé**, you will arrive at the important pulp and paper town of **Donnacona**.

Donnacona (Population 3,500). Here, at the high-level bridge, there is a most interesting view of **a pulp mill in action**, with huge piles of logs and acres of bark refuse.

The name Donnacona belonged, originally, to the Indian who ruled over the land on which the city of Quebec now stands, which Parkman described as "The hamlet of Stadaconé, with its king, Donnacona, and its naked lords and princes." In 1536, Jacques Cartier treacherously captured Donnacona and took him to France as a living proof that his fabulous tales of adventure and discovery were true. Cartier referred to Donnacona as "the lord of Canada", one of the earliest recorded uses of the name "Canada".

The town of Donnacona, besides its pulp and paper industry, has a number of shops, a movie and a golf course.

The road now passes through farming country, and the picturesque villages of Les Ecureuils, which means "the squirrels", and Neuville which, in spite of its name, is another very old farming community. This is a good place to buy **maple syrup and maple sugar**.

At **St-Augustin**, on a clear day, there is an impressive vista of the mountains to the north, a glimpse of the beauties that are yet to come. Six miles beyond you will be at the crossroads leading to the city of Quebec. Route 2 will take you by way of Ste-Foy to the Upper Town, while Route 2C leads to Lower Town. By either road you have about eight miles more to go. There is **a Tourist Information Bureau** near the crossroads, and it is not a bad idea to stop there to ask the way and get a map of the city of Quebec.

Chapter 8

THE CITY OF QUEBEC

Quebec (Population 200,000). We have come, at last, to Canada's oldest and most romantic city. Here is romance in its purest sense. Picturesque in appearance, its language sprung from a Latin origin, in spirit and in mood it reminds us of a medieval tale of chivalry. Here is adventure which, to many of you, will seem more or less remote from ordinary life. It is romantic, too, in the sense that it has an imaginative and poetic quality, tending away from the sanity of classicism to medieval forms.

Quebec has another quality, one which it shares to a certain extent with the entire province. Its people are bound by ancient ties to the Roman Catholic Church and to the French language. The bond is so strong that it is not merely an adjunct or an attribute of French Canadian life, it is life itself.

We can think of no city that has been photographed, described and extolled more than the city of Quebec. To do it justice one must use superlatives. For that very reason there is the possibility of a feeling of anti-climax when you first see it. Some people experience this let-down, especially when they make the mistake of trying to see everything in a short space of time by wandering aimlessly about, or by driving, without a guide, through the narrow crowded streets.

Quebec has taken three hundred and fifty years to grow. It can not be seen in an hour.

The feeling of anti-climax can turn to one of irritation

if you have not taken the precaution to make reservations. During July and August the hotels are usually crowded. On the day of Sainte Anne more than fifty thousand people pour into the city and fill to overflowing every hotel and rooming house from Quebec to Ste-Anne-de-Beaupré. To avoid disappointment, it is not only desirable but necessary to secure a room well in advance of your arrival.

We have been criticized, occasionally, for placing too much emphasis on hotels and not enough on scenery. Personally, we cannot enjoy the most gorgeous sunset that ever splashed its red and gold across a sky if we are wandering in a vain attempt to find a place to sleep.

We are not unique. Most travellers are restless and vaguely unhappy in a strange city until they have found satisfactory accommodations. Once you have unpacked your bag and settled at the hotel of your choice, your whole mental attitude changes. You no longer feel stranded. You live somewhere. You become a part of the picture. You belong. At the end of a tiring but happy day you think of your comfortable hotel room and you say: "It's time to go home." And so we urge a little forethought, especially in Quebec, so that all housing difficulties will be avoided.

The hotel of your choice! Which shall it be?

At the top of every list you will inevitably find the Château Frontenac, one of the world's most famous hotels. It stands on historic ground. Here was Champlain's fort in 1620, and the Château St-Louis, residence of the early French governors. The hotel is reminiscent of that ancient château. It rises above Cap-Diamant like a great medieval castle. Far beneath it lies Lower Town, where ghosts of the past seem to wander at night in the shadow of the great rock.

Flanking the Château is Dufferin Terrace, a gay promenade in the summer, and the scene of winter sports when the snow falls. **The coffee shop** overlooks the terrace and opens onto it. The main entrance to the hotel is from Rue St-Louis and the Place d'Armes.

Behind the Château Frontenac is the Governor's Garden, laid out by Governor Montmagny in 1647. Historic names are everywhere. The hotel was called after Count Frontenac, who came to Canada in 1672 to be Governor of New France, under King Louis XIV. You may dance every evening in the Jacques Cartier room, named after the discoverer of Quebec. You may have tea each afternoon in the dignified drawing-room called after Champlain. The cocktail lounge is known as the Frontenac Room. From all these rooms, and from many of the bedrooms, there is a magnificent panorama encompassing Lévis, the Island of Orleans, and the St. Lawrence River.

If this is your first visit to Quebec, by all means stay at the Château Frontenac. No other hotel in the city can compare with it. In spite of its size you will find here a quiet charm and an air of luxurious comfort. Its grandeur is unobtrusive. The rates vary, according to the accommodation and outlook, from reasonable to prohibitive.

This is the very core and centre of Quebec. You could not be in a more convenient location.

If you are averse to grandeur and would rather be in a smaller and less expensive hotel, you might like the Clarendon, on Rue Ste-Anne, opposite the City Hall, within a block of the Place d'Armes. Although it is an old-time commercial hotel, it has been completely renovated and remodelled so that every room now has a private bath. Its dining room has a good reputation. We found it quite satisfactory.

Another modernized commercial hotel, popular with tourists, is the Hotel St-Louis, quite close to the Château Frontenac, on Rue St-Louis. Here, too, every room has its own bath and there is an air-conditioned dining room upstairs which is quiet and cool on a hot day. Rates are reasonable at both the Clarendon and the St-Louis Hotels.

Perhaps your choice would be **a small and quiet place outside the city walls**, where traffic is less congested and parking is easy at any time. If so, the Habitant Inn, 525 St. Foy Road (Chemin Ste-Foy) is probably just what you want. In spite of its name, this inn is run by English people. It is set far back from the road in its own spacious grounds, and at first glance it appears to be a private house. There is a "tea-room" simplicity to its furnishings and to its dining room. Some of the bedrooms have private baths. It is entirely unpretentious, but we enjoyed waking in the morning to the song of birds outside our window, and it was a delight to be able to park our car in the large yard with no fuss and bother. Rates are moderate.

Sometimes when we are visiting Quebec, we **live in the country and drive in each day**. There are several quite charming places which we like very much, within fifteen miles or less of the city.

Our choice is the Manoir St-Castin, at Lac Beauport, a thousand feet up in the mountains, and **a delightful resort summer or winter**. It used to take us about half an hour to drive in to town on Highway 54. We thought the meals were particularly good, French cooking at its best. We liked our room with its view across the pretty fresh water lake. In summer the swimming is fine, either at the sand beach or from the broad deck of the Nautical Club. Tennis is popular, as it is all over Quebec. Boats and canoes are there for you to use, night and day.

In winter you will find some of **the best skiing in the Quebec region** right at the door of the Manoir St-Castin. An Alpine Ski Lift will take you to the top of a twenty-five hundred foot run, and there are also rope tows. The hotel is quite reminiscent of a French Swiss resort, cozy and warm in winter, cool and airy in summer. Considering the quality, we thought the rates were reasonable.

Also within easy motoring distance of the city, is the Château Bel-Air, at Sainte-Pétronille on the Island of Orleans. We will tell you about the island later. If you like to live right beside the river, almost as if you were on a boat, you will be happy at the Château Bel-Air. It is an old hotel, patronized mostly by French Canadians from Quebec. It has been well kept up, with fresh paint in pretty colour schemes, and the bedrooms are comfortably furnished in habitant style. We thought the meals were very nice and the rates reasonable.

You can swim from the hotel verandah when the tide is in, and Ste-Pétronille's pleasant 9 hole golf course is within easy walking distance.

At night you can sit on one of the long verandahs and look across the river at the lights of the city of Quebec and watch the ships passing.

The beautiful bridge from Montmorency to the Ile d'Orléans brings the Château Bel-Air within half an hour's drive of the city, via the new wide Highway 15.

Not far from the bridge, at Montmorency Falls, is Kent House, a house built around **the historic home of Queen Victoria's father**, the Duke of Kent. Kent House Hotel is advertised as a resort but we would call it a "sight-seeing hotel", and we do not mean to imply that

Above) Manoir St-Castin, Lac Beauport—French Cooking at its Best
(*Below*) Looking Down Rue St-Louis, Quebec

it is anything but delightful. Its dining room, overlooking the famous Montmorency Falls, has good meals, and most of the bedrooms are quite pleasing.

The championship course of the Royal Quebec Golf Club is only five minutes away. Other sports are available on the grounds. However, it is not a resort in our sense of the word because most of the guests are sightseers who come for a day or two and move on. There is not much social life around the hotel during the summer season, but it is a first rate place to live while you visit the Shrine of Ste-Anne-de-Beaupré, fourteen miles away, or while you explore the historic sites around Quebec, seven miles distant.

The main part of the house was originally built about 1778 as a country place for General Sir Frederick Haldimand, Governor of Canada. There is a romantic story about the Duke of Kent living here from 1791 to 1794 with his lady love. When he returned to England, he married and became the father of the future Queen Victoria.

We like this hotel best when it is out of season, which means any time except July and August. We thought the room rates rather high, but after all there is only one Kent House and only one Montmorency Falls and the combination is well worth seeing.

If you decide to stay at the Château Frontenac, or at one of the other hotels in the city, be sure to drive out to Kent House for lunch or dinner in **the delightful dining pavillion overlooking the falls**.

All the hotels we have mentioned have dining rooms and they will all welcome you for meals, even if you are staying somewhere else. There are also a great many restaurants in Quebec, ranging all the way from adequate

(*Above*) Kent House, Montmorency Falls, the Historic Home of Queen Victoria's Father   (*Below*) A French Canadian Calèche at the Place d'Armes, Quebec

to superb. In general we found the food interesting, well
prepared and reasonably priced.

Of the **restaurants**, Kerhulu's is probably **the most
distinctive**. It is in the centre of the shopping district of
Upper Town, 22 Rue de la Fabrique, which runs along
one side of the Parc de l'Hôtel de Ville (City Hall Park).
Kerhulu's Restaurant is under the same management as
the Manoir St-Castin and it has the same high quality
of French cooking. In appearance this restaurant is an
odd combination of cake shop and cocktail bar. The
elaborate menu includes many unusual dishes which
appeal to epicures. Expensive, but worth it.

Another of our favourites is Chez Marino Restaurant,
35 Rue Dauphine, just outside the old city walls, near
the Provincial Parliament Buildings. Marino's specializes
in Italian food such as ragotini and spaghetti, but the
menu is varied and contains French and English dishes,
too. The prices are reasonable, and you may have lunch
or dinner at any time from noon until midnight.

Practically all the hotels and restaurants in Quebec
have cocktail bars, and serve wine or beer with meals, if
desired.

Before you begin a sight-seeing programme, there are
two other things you should know: where to get further
information, and where to park your car.

Information. A branch of **the Tourist Bureau** of the
Province of Quebec is ready to help you with information
and excellent maps of the city and province. You will
find it at **106 Grande-Allée**, not far from the Parliament
Buildings.

If you are thinking of taking a fishing trip through
the Parc des Laurentides, be sure to make arrangements

for your camp accommodations while you are in the city of Quebec. The Tourist Bureau will give you the necessary information.

Parking. This is always a major problem in big cities, but it is not as difficult here as you might imagine, considering the intricacies of handling traffic on such narrow and winding streets. You may park for half an hour in front of the Tourist Bureau on the Grande-Allée in a space reserved for out of town cars. For a longer period, there is a large free parking area on the Esplanade, just inside the old city walls, near the St. Louis Gate.

We often found vacant spaces to park in front of the City Hall, around the Parliament Buildings, and at the Parc Montmorency near the Post Office.

No over-night parking is allowed on the city streets.

Before you go "home" to the hotel of your choice, why not join the promenade on Dufferin Terrace? If it is summer there will probably be a band concert. In winter the famous toboggan slide will be the centre of attraction. Here you can get a panoramic view of the sights we are to see tomorrow. You can look down on the oldest part of Quebec, where Champlain built his *Habitation* in 1608. As you walk along the boardwalk you will be treading on the ancient walls of the Château St-Louis. You can look up at that once formidable fortress, the Citadel, where the past and present meet, for during the Quebec Conference of 1943 Winston Churchill and Franklin D. Roosevelt stayed in the Citadel. Officially it is the Quebec residence of the Governor-General of Canada.

You can see Cap-Diamant, rising to a height of three hundred and sixty feet above the St. Lawrence River and stretching for seven miles along the shoreline, and you can look across at the skyline of Lévis, lovely at night when its lights seem to vie with the stars.

As you stroll along Dufferin Terrace you will pass close to the three hundred year old Governor's Garden, and you will pause, no doubt, to look at the monument erected there in 1828 to the two heroes of the Battle of the Plains of Abraham—the English General Wolfe and the French General Montcalm. It was an English victory in 1759, but when one remembers that less than seven hundred years before this the French had conquered England, and had remained there to rule as kings, the question arises as to who conquered whom on the Plains of Abraham. The truth is, although few are willing to admit it, that the French and English Canadians sprang from mixtures of the same Norman stock. Their differences are those of language and religion, not of race. On basic issues, if the freedom of Canada is threatened, the differences disappear in a strong national unity.

As you walk up and down the boardwalk you will no longer feel like a visitor in a strange city. You will become a part of the picturesque parade, and slowly but surely the charm of Quebec will wrap itself around you. As for us, whenever we see this view from Dufferin Terrace we agree most heartily with Count Frontenac who wrote of it in 1672: "I never saw anything more superb than the position of this town".

Sight-seeing. No one can plan the perfect sight-seeing tour for anyone else. It is an individual thing, subject to moods and personal interests. However, it may be helpful if we tell you how we did it, and you may follow us or not as you please.

We separated Quebec into areas, as follows:

(1) Lower Town.
(2) The City within the Walls.
(3) The City beyond the Walls.

This arrangement allowed us to see things in approximately chronological order, with two notable exceptions. The Jesuit Mission at Sillery, the oldest house still standing in Quebec, is beyond the city limits, and the ancient General Hospital, which was a Récollet farm in 1620, is far beyond the walls, up the St. Charles River.

There are a few other minor exceptions, but we found that history came alive for us, and fell into its proper place and period surprisingly well, when we began our sight-seeing tour at the Place Royale in Lower Town.

Lower Town. The French call it Ville-en-bas, or Basse-Ville. It goes back to the founding of Quebec by Champlain. An incline elevator will take you down the steep cliff of Cap-Diamant from Dufferin Terrace, or you may walk down the "Breakneck Steps" to Rue Sous-le-Fort and that tiny square of land so steeped in history, the Place Royale.

The story of Quebec really begins with its discovery by Jacques Cartier in 1535. He found on this site the Iroquois Indian village of Stadacona, capital of a domain ruled over by the Indian Chief Donnacona, and called by the savages "The Kingdom of Canada". The name Canada is believed to be a corruption of an Iroquois word meaning a village, or collection of huts.

To the east was "The Kingdom of the Saguenay", and to the west was Hochelaga, where Montreal now stands. When Champlain came here, seventy-three years later, no trace remained of Stadacona.

Champlain and his twenty-eight settlers arrived at

Quebec on the third of July, 1608. They anchored off Cap-Diamant and went ashore to find a suitable place to build. In describing it, Champlain wrote: "I could find no place more convenient or better situated than the point of Quebec, so called by the savages." Here he built his habitation on the Place Royale, which in those days was on the bank of the river. He planted gardens all around it. There were three buildings two stories high, the largest of which was the storehouse, 36 feet long.

Champlain's church stood on Sous-le-Fort, at the foot of the Breakneck Steps. It was destroyed during the first English occupation of Quebec, from 1629 to 1632.

The present Church of Notre-Dame-des-Victoires, facing the Place Royale, was built in 1688. Only the walls are the original. The roof and the interior were burned during the siege of Quebec in 1759, the year of the Battle of the Plains of Abraham. This charming little church is **one of the city's earliest buildings** that is still in use. Originally it was called L'Enfant-Jésus, but the name was changed to Norte-Dame-de-Victoire after the victory over Admiral Sir William Phips in 1690. The plural, "Des Victoires" was added after the failure of Sir Hovenden Walker's naval expedition, sent in 1711 to put an end to French rule in Canada.

The square in front of the church was **Quebec's earliest market place**. All around it stood the houses of the merchants. In the centre a bronze bust of King Louis XIV of France was erected in Frontenac's time, but it was removed later because the merchants complained that it interfered with traffic. The present bust of King Louis commemorates the original.

In a corner of the Place Royale, opposite the church, a plaque has been placed on the traditional site where

Hélène, the young wife of Governor Champlain, used to teach the Indian children. Tradition also says that she wore a mirror around her neck on a chain, and when the Indians saw the reflections of their faces in the glass, they believed that she always carried their pictures in her heart.

Hélène had married Champlain in Paris in 1610, but as she was only twelve years old at the time, she did not come to live with him in Canada until ten years later. During the four years she lived in Quebec, the Place Royale was the centre of the small settlement.

Louis Hébert and his wife, Canada's first farmers, had moved to Quebec from Acadia in 1617, and had cleared a farm on the heights. A few years later Champlain built his stone fort on the cliff, but during Madame Champlain's sojourn in Canada, the town of Quebec remained below, in the narrow space between the rock and the river.

The low stone building next to the present Hotel Louis XIV on the Place Royale, was the first home of the Ursuline Order of Nuns of New France. They came to Canada in 1639 to establish a school for Indian girls. Madame de La Peltrie, who founded the convent, was the same courageous lady who, three years later, went to Ville-Marie to help Maisonneuve establish his settlement on the Island of Montreal. The Ursulines leased this house on the Place Royale from one of the merchants. It was their school and their home until they moved, in 1642, into their "new" convent on the heights adjoining the Hébert farm, where they have remained ever since.

The first Mother Superior of the Ursulines was that remarkable woman, the Venerable Marie de l'Incarnation. Widowed at nineteen, she devoted the rest of her life to teaching the savages and organizing schools for girls. Her numerous letters to her son give a vivid picture of life in Quebec during the seventeenth century.

"The fort is of stone," she wrote, "as are its out-buildings. The houses of the Reverend Fathers, of the Foundress of the Hospitalière Nuns, and of the Indians who have settled here are also built of stone. Some of the Indians live in portable birchbark houses, which they put up very skillfully on poles."

Unfortunately, a series of disastrous fires have destroyed many of the old stone houses. Others have been torn down in the path of progress. Some remain, and as you wander through the narrow streets of oldest Quebec, it is not too difficult to conjure up the life of those earliest days of the French regime.

On Sunday, Lower Town is practically deserted and it is the best day to prowl about, digging into history. On week days the traffic problem is terrific, but on Sunday you will have no difficulty finding a place to park on the very spot where Champlain moored his ships in 1608. If you are driving your own car, the best way to get from Upper to Lower Town is to start from the Place d'Armes in front of the Château Frontenac, go along Du-Fort, turn right between the old Post Office and the Parc Montmorency, and down the Côte de la Montagne.

The oldest cemetery in Quebec, where many of the early settlers are buried, lies just below the Parc Montmorency. Abraham Martin, farmer and pilot was buried here in 1664. His thirty-two acres on the heights became known as "the plains of Abraham".

Under the cliff, below the old cemetery, there is a street with the quaint name of Sault-au-Matelot. A barricade at the end of this street was the scene of fierce fighting during the night of General Montgomery's

MONTMORENCY FALLS
Higher than Niagara.

attack, in 1775. Here French and English Canadians united, for the first time, to fight a common enemy.

Beyond Sault-au-Matelot is Sous-le-Cap. Described as "the narrowest street in America", it is more colourful in pictures than in reality.

After a surfeit of sight-seeing, **a boat trip is cool and restful**, and Quebec looks dramatic from the middle of the river.

The Lévis ferries, carrying passengers and cars, run continuously all day from a wharf near the foot of Sous-le-Fort Street. For **a longer cruise** you might like one of the Quebec Waterways Sightseeing Tours. Their ticket office is next to the Lévis Ferry Dock. The morning boat goes to Ste-Anne-de-Beaupré. The afternoon trip will take you up the river as far as the Quebec bridge and down to see the Montmorency Falls. Every evening, rain or shine, there is a so-called "Moonlight Cruise".

The City Within the Walls. It is hardly necessary to outline for you the area of the walled city. The fortifications still stand, almost intact, and to leave the confines of the old city you must either climb down the cliff or pass through one of the old stone gates.

The original walls were begun under the French in 1703, and they cost so much that King Louis XIV is said to have asked if the fortifications at Quebec were built of gold. All the walls were reconstructed by the British in 1823. Today they are obsolete, but they are an eloquent reminder of the long struggle between the French, the English, and the Indians for supremacy in the New World.

By far the most picturesque and exciting way to see this part of the city is to take one of the **horse-drawn vehicles**, either an English victoria or a French Canadian *calèche*. They are lined up at the Place d'Armes in front of the Château Frontenac waiting for passengers. The driver will act as your guide, and will give you a commentary, either in English or in French, as you jog along.

The distances are not great, and here is an itinerary if you would rather walk. A good starting point is the Champlain Monument, on Dufferin Terrace. Although Champlain seems to belong more completely to the Lower Town, he died on the heights in 1635, in Fort St-Louis, where his monument now stands.

Walk across the Place d'Armes Square, which the French sometimes call the Rond-de-Chênes. In the centre of the square the **Faith Monument** commemorates the Récollets who came to Quebec in 1615, the first religious order to attempt the conversion of the Indians.

Beyond the square, at 22 Rue Ste-Anne, stands the Vallée House, one of the real old-timers. It was the home of Martin Boutet who came to Canada in 1640, and was professor of mathematics at the old Jesuit College. Louis Jolliet, discoverer of the Upper Mississippi, was probably among his pupils. The old house is now the **Musée Historique**, an interesting collection of life-sized wax figures in scenes that depict the history of Canada.

Across the street from the Vallée house, in a walled garden, stands **the Anglican Cathedral of the Holy Trinity**, built in 1804. The Royal pew, of English oak, is occupied by the Governor-General and his family when they are in residence at the Citadel. King George III presented the silver communion set, engraved with the royal arms.

Just beyond the English Cathedral, where the City Hall now stands, was **the farm of Louis Hébert**, Champlain's friend and first settler. A monument to his memory marks the approximate location of his farm house, which was built of stone and was thirty-eight feet long. The statue was erected to commemorate the third centennial of Hébert's arrival in Quebec.

Turn down Rue des Jardins, where gardens used to bloom, and on Buade Street you will see **the handsome Basilica de Notre-Dame**. This is the Roman Catholic Cathedral of the archdiocese of Quebec. Its records go back to 1647. Monseigneur de Laval, Canada's first Bishop, consecrated it in 1666. The present building was erected after the fire of 1922, on the original walls.

Next to the Basilica, through a quaint iron gateway, you will find the old Quebec Seminary, founded by Bishop de Laval in 1663, and **Laval University**, its direct descendant, built in 1852. **The museum and art gallery** are well worth seeing.

You are now in the heart of **the fashionable shopping district**, Rue de la Fabrique. When you are hungry the famous Kerhulu's Restaurant is only a step away.

At the opposite end of Buade Street is the Post Office, built on the site of the house of Nicolas Jacquin called Philibert in the story of *Le Chien d'Or*. The well known "Golden Dog" stone has been set above the Buade Street entrance of the Post Office. It was originally above the door of the Philibert house to defy the tyranny of the infamous Intendant Bigot. In a free translation, the stone reads:

> I AM A DOG THAT IS GNAWING A BONE
> WHILE I GNAW IT, I CROUCH ALONE.
> THE TIME WILL COME, WHICH HAS NOT COME YET,
> WHEN I SHALL BITE HIM BY WHOM I'VE BEEN BIT.

The interesting story of the times of the Intendant Bigot has been retold in *The Golden Dog*, an historical romance by one of Canada's earliest novelists, William Kirby.

In front of the Post Office is a monument to Bishop Laval, and opposite, through stone gates, is the Archbishop's Palace. The park on the edge of the cliff, overlooking Lower Town, is **Parc Montmorency**, a pleasant place to sit and rest. Here stood the old Parliament House where the Quebec conference was held which resulted in the Confederation of Canada in 1867.

Follow the old wall along the Rue des Remparts which, as its name implies, was originally part of the fortifications on the embankment. This is an interesting walk and there is a good view of the Beauport shore, the Island of Orleans, and the waterfront.

There are a number of two-hundred-year-old houses along the embankment, among them the house called **Candiac** at 47 Rue des Remparts where General Montcalm lived from 1758 until his death the following year at the Battle of the Plains of Abraham.

If you look over the wall of the Ramparts at this spot you will be looking down on the Côte de la Canoterie, which means the canoe landing hill. In the days of the voyageurs and fur traders, the river came almost to the foot of this cliff. The land beyond has since been reclaimed.

Behind the high wall which now flanks the Rue des Remparts and fronts on Palace Hill, is the ancient and honoured building of the **Hôtel-Dieu Hospital**. It was founded by the Duchesse d'Aiguillon who was a niece of Cardinal Richelieu. The Hospitalière Nuns came to Quebec in 1639, the same year as the Ursuline Nuns. The hospital, which was built at that time, is still standing and in use, although additions have been made and it has been modernized. The museum of the Hôtel-Dieu contains seventeenth century books, furniture and silver. There are several celebrated paintings in the chapel, including *The Vision of St. Thérèse.*

There is a break in the old walls at Palace Hill to allow motor traffic to pass up and down. Originally this road was barred by the Palace Gate. Beyond, on the lower level, stood the Intendant's Palace and the King's Brewery. Talon, the first Intendant—King Louis' agent in New France—was alarmed by the amount of brandy the people were drinking, and believing that beer would be less harmful, he built a brewery in 1668. Boswell's Brewery stands on the same site, and still uses the original vaults.

A Dominion Arsenal occupies the north-west bastion of the old fortifications, but you can by-pass it by going up Palace Hill to Rue St-Jean. This is **a busy shopping street** and one of the city's main thoroughfares. If you follow it to the walls you will come to Porte St-Jean, a reconstruction of one of the old city gates. Going south inside the walls, along Rue d'Auteuil and the Esplanade, you will pass the other remaining gates, Kent and St. Louis. The St. Louis Gate is probably the best known, most photographed, and most characteristic of all the landmarks of Quebec.

A short distance beyond the St. Louis Gate the old walls end at **the Citadel**, the most impressive of all the fortifications built by the British in 1823. The main entrance is behind the Garrison Club, through the Dalhousie Gate.

The Rue St-Louis, which will bring you back to your starting point on Dufferin Terrace, is **one of the most interesting streets in Quebec**. About two hundred years ago it was the city's fashionable residential district. Many of the houses date from that time, or earlier. The villainous Angélique of the "Golden Dog" story, Madame de Péan, friend of the Intendant Bigot, lived at number 59 Rue St-Louis.

Nearly opposite is the narrow Rue du Parloir, which leads to the ancient Convent of the Ursulines. You will remember that these Nuns lived in Lower Town, at the Place Royale, when they arrived at Quebec in 1639. The building of this "new" convent is recorded in the *Jesuit Relations* of 1642:

> This seminary is one of the fairest ornaments in the colony and a great help in the detention and the conversion of the savages. The Sisters moved to their new dwelling, leaving the one they had leased on the twenty-first of November, 1642. The building is large and substantial, and well and carefully constructed.

It must indeed have been well built, for in spite of two fires and the ravages of over three hundred years the original walls still remain in the inner cloister.

Returning to St. Louis Street, you will notice **an odd little house with a high-pitched roof** opposite the St. Louis Hotel. It was built almost three hundred years ago and is the so-called Montcalm House, although the General never lived there.

The Duke of Kent's town house was number 23 Rue St-Louis. The first two stories of this building date from the middle of the seventeenth century. It was here that de Ramezay signed the Capitulation of Quebec, on September 18th, 1759, and the French regime officially ended in the city.

And now we have arrived back at the Place d'Armes, Dufferin Terrace and the Château Frontenac.

As an antidote to so much sight-seeing, may we suggest a short drive in the country? How about driving out Highway 54 to Lac Beauport for a swim, or for a paddle on the lake, and top off the evening with one of the delicious dinners at the Manoir St-Castin?

Tomorrow we shall explore the city beyond the walls, which can all be done, without any difficulty, in your car.

Beyond the Walls. There are three points of historic interest outside the city walls which we know you will not want to miss. One is the old Récollet house and farm, which stood on the St. Charles River in 1620 and now is a part of the General Hospital. Another is the oldest house in Canada, built at Sillery in 1637 as a Jesuit Indian Mission. The third is the Plains of Abraham, now known as the Parc des Champs de Bataille.

Although these three places are some distance apart, they can be incorporated into an interesting drive which will take you through many of the beautiful residential districts of the city and suburbs.

Leave by the St. John Gate, follow the Côte d'Abraham down the hill and turn right on Rue de la Couronne (Hy. 54). This is the St-Roch district, which has its own shopping street, Rue St-Joseph, and seems almost like another city. At the Marché St-Roch turn left on Rue Gignac and cross the bridge to Victoria Park. The baseball stadium is here, and a children's playground.

Drive across the park to the Parent Bridge. From this side of the St. Charles River there is a good view of the buildings of the General Hospital, behind the ancient cloister walls.

No building in Quebec is more interesting historically and architecturally. In the summer of 1620 the Récollets built a stone house on this spot, with outworks for defence, and cleared the land for a farm. Their live stock consisted of a pair of asses, several hogs, some geese, fowl and ducks. At that time the only other farmer in the entire colony was Louis Hébert, on the heights.

The Récollets built a cell in their house. It still exists and gives the exact location of the original building, now incorporated within the hospital walls.

The hospital was founded by Mgr. de St-Vallier, the second bishop of Quebec, who placed it in charge of the Hospitalière Nuns in 1692.

In spite of his good deeds, the austere Bishop St-Vallier is probably best remembered for his quarrels with the Governor, Count Frontenac. To cheer the colony during the long winter and to celebrate the arrival of furs from the upper lakes, Frontenac decided to produce private theatricals at the Château St-Louis. The Bishop issued a mandate denouncing the plays as "impious, impure and noxious comedies". The conflict spread until it involved almost everyone in the settlement. The Canadian playwright, Robertson Davies, uses the incident in his play, *Hope Deferred*.

But to return to the General Hospital. The buildings are a fine example of seventeenth century Canadian construction and design. Some of the walls appear to be built of boards, but on closer inspection we found they were actually of stone, about two feet thick, the clapboards being used merely as a facing.

A somewhat similar construction has been used on the old Jesuit Mission, at Sillery, our next objective. The Boulevard Langelier, which begins at the General Hospital gates, will take you to the foot of a very steep hill. Climb this to de Salaberry Avenue, and turn right on the Chemin Ste-Foy. This is a charming residential street, with some beautiful old houses.

If you pause for a moment in the **Monument des Braves Park** and look towards the mountains, you will see how the city of Quebec has grown to the north, for many miles beyond the St. Charles River. The monument in the park is dedicated to the Chevalier de Lévis, General Murray, and the brave men, French and English, who fought in the battle of Ste-Foy. It was erected a hundred years after the battle, by the Saint-Jean-Baptiste Society of Quebec, and is another symbol of the growing unity between the two races.

The Avenue des Braves, a charming residential street will bring you to the St. Louis Road (not to be confused with the Rue St-Louis within the walls).

A few hundred yards away, in Sillery, is Bois de Coulonge, formerly Spencerwood, originally the old "Chatellenie de Coulonge" granted in 1657 to Governor D'Ailleboust. After Confederation Lord Elgin lived there as Governor-General. It is now **the official residence of the Lieutenant-Governor of Quebec**. It stands in a large heavily wooded park overlooking the St. Lawrence River and can not be seen from the highway.

Follow the St. Louis Road until you come to the Côte de l'Eglise, a steep hill which will take you down to the river level and to **the oldest house in Canada**. It stands at number 2320 on a quaint, winding street called the Chemin des Foulons. In the summer of 1637 six labourers began the stone work for this building, the Indian Mission House of Saint-Joseph de Sillery.

One of the founders of the Mission was Paul Le Jeune, Superior of the Jesuit Mission at Quebec, and author of many of the *Relations*, those remarkable books which were, to a large extent, responsible for the influx of missionaries and nuns to the wilderness of Canada. When Champlain, the Father of New France, died in his

(*Above*) THE GENERAL HOSPITAL FOUNDED IN 1692 IS INTERESTING
HISTORICALLY AND ARCHITECTURALLY (*Below*) THE JESUIT
MISSION OF SILLERY IS THE OLDEST HOUSE IN CANADA

fort at Quebec on Christmas day, 1635, it was Father
Jeune who pronounced his eulogy.

Two years after the death of Champlain, Father
Jeune took possession of the new stone house at Sille
which we have come down to see. It administered to
Algonquin Indians. A stone church was built across
street, where a monument now stands, and not far aw
there was a Hôtel-Dieu Hospital.

The Mission Register contains some of the m
famous names in the early history of Canada: Maiso
neuve, Jeanne Mance and Madame de La Peltrie,
their way up the river to found Montreal; the Jes
Martyrs, Saint Jean de Brébeuf and Saint Gabriel La
mant, friends of Father Le Jeune, and a great ma
others. This old mission house, which has been carefu
repaired, is truly a link with Canada's heroic past.

If you have the time, you might like to run out to
the Quebec Bridge, about three miles beyond Sillery
masterpiece of engineering. We will be crossing it, la
on, when we leave for the south shore.

Another famous spot, about two miles upstream fr
the bridge, is Cap-Rouge, now nothing but a small su
mer settlement at the mouth of the Cap-Rouge Riv
but in Jacques Cartier's time the site of the ill-fat
attempts of Cartier and Roberval to establish a colo
in the New World.

On your way back to the city, from Sillery, it
interesting to drive along close to the river, past t
Quebec Yacht Club to Anse Aux Foulons. This is
historic Wolfe's Cove. Nearby are the wharves of
Canadian Pacific Steamship Company, built on
claimed land.

A very steep road climbs up the cliff at almost t
exact spot where Wolfe's army scaled the heights befo

the battle. At the top of this road you will be on the Plains of Abraham or, as it is now called, the Parc des Champs de Bataille, **a National Battlefields Park**. A beautiful driveway runs through it, circling all the historic sites, which are marked by monuments or stones. The Earl Grey Terrace, a look-out above Wolfe's Cove, was named after Canada's Governor-General who inaugurated the park in 1908, just three hundred years after the founding of Quebec by Champlain.

Before you leave the Plains of Abraham, be sure to visit **the Provincial Museum**, housed in a handsome modern building. There are some models of the old Quebec houses, several volumes of the *Jesuit Relations* and many other rare and interesting historical treasures. There is also an exhibit of native birds and animals, including a collection made by Abbé Provancher, for whom the Provancher Society of Natural History of Canada was named.

When you leave, turn right on the Grande-Allée, a wide and beautiful residential street which will take you back to the St. Louis Gate.

The impressive stone building facing the old city walls and towering high above them is the Hôtel du Gouvernement which houses the **Provincial Parliament**. It is an outstanding example of mid-Victorian Renaissance architecture. The interior is noteworthy, especially the Legislative Chambers, with their interesting paintings of historic scenes. Statues of famous Canadian heroes adorn the façade, many of them the work of the renowned Canadian sculptor, Philippe Hébert. Other notable statues are in the well-kept grounds.

If you are hungry at this point, Marino's Restaurant is just across the park, on Dauphine Street.

There is more to Quebec—much more; the many fine

churches; the Zoo; the Indians of Lorette—but we believe that we have told you about the most interesting and important sights to be seen in and near the city. When you have seen them all, at your leisure, we should like to take you across the long bridge from Montmorency to the lovely, rural Ile d'Orléans. Or do you always think of it as the Island of Orleans?

Chapter 9

THE ISLAND OF ORLEANS

WHEN JACQUES CARTIER ANCHORED his ship beside it in 1535, he called it the Island of Bacchus, because the trees were thickly hung with grapes. After more than four hundred years the fertile soil still produces fine fruits and vegetables.

There was no bridge to the mainland until the summer of 1935. Before that a ferry ran during the navigation season, and the people drove over the ice in the winter time. This semi-isolation kept Ile d'Orléans separated in spirit from the city of Quebec and gave it a unique quality of its own.

Today the graceful suspension bridge has changed all that by bringing the ancient farm houses within twenty minutes' motoring distance of the heart of the city. As the island is only twenty miles long and about five miles wide, and as the highway around it is less than 50 miles long, it can easily be covered in an afternoon's drive.

However, if you want to know it as it really is, and to sense its unusual tempo and mood, we think you should live there, for a short time at least. If you do this, we are sure you will love it.

There is the smell of the sea and there are tides at the Ile d'Orléans. There is the smell of the good earth, too, wind-swept and clean and free of the contamination of heavy industry. On our first visit, we were impressed by the greenness of the countryside, and by the simple beauty of the churches and the farm houses, many of which are more than two hundred years old.

As you climb up the steep hill that leads from the bridge, and drive to the resort village of Ste-Pétronille, you will pass close to where St-Roch left the imprint of his foot in the rock, in the days when the legendary witches inhabited the island.

Ste-Pétronilie is the only village on Ile d'Orléans that makes a serious attempt to cater to visitors. We had always been told that it was a "primitive" place, and "too, too quaint". We were, therefore, amazed to find such **a comfortable inn** as the Château Bel-Air, which we told you about in the chapter on the City of Quebec. It stands on the river's brink, beside the old ferry wharf, which is now used as a parking area.

Another surprise was the **Orleans Golf Club**, within walking distance of the Château Bel-Air. It has a nine hole course with some lovely views, and a small Victorian club house which serves sandwiches and drinks.

In and around the village there are a number of large country places, many of which have tennis courts and beautiful gardens. On the winding main street, the cottages of the French regime have been kept in good repair and are mostly occupied by summer residents from Quebec. One of these old cottages, near the hotel, takes paying guests.

Still another surprise was in store for us as we drove down the island. A number of the prosperous farms have modern tractors, telephones and electric light. The Ile d'Orléans farmers have adopted what is good from the present without sacrificing the traditions of their historic past.

St-Laurent. Ship building, with its subsidiaries, yacht repairing and winter quarters for boats, is the principal industry in this village, which lies about six miles down

STE-PÉTRONILLE, ISLAND OF ORLEANS
The Château Bel-Air stands on the river brink.

the river from Ste-Pétronille. There are some lovely old world farm houses surrounded by fruit trees and market gardens, among them the Pouliot farm, which has bee in the family since 1665. The seventeenth century gris mill, beside a pretty waterfall, is picturesque.

A sign in the village reads:

WOLFE CAME ASHORE AT ST-LAURENT
ON THE ISLAND OF ORLEANS
ON THE 27TH OF JULY 1759.

On that occasion the parish priest posted a petitio on the door of the church addressed to "The brav officers of the English army", asking them to spare h beloved church and presbytery. Wolfe, according to th story, was so moved by the request, and by the dignit of the old priest, that he not only spared the church bu offered to pay for the building of an annex to the pre bytery.

Along the shore of the river there are a great man private summer cottages, while on the opposite side c the road there are prosperous farms. About seven mil farther down the island we came to the Plage d'Orléan **a beach and swimming pool** beside the river, with bat houses and tennis courts.

St-Jean. All the villages have charm, but this on appealed to us particularly, partly because of the ir teresting old **Manoir Mauvide-Genest**, a fine example c a seventeenth century seigneurie. The house, which seventy-five feet long and twenty-five feet wide, wa completely restored and the small chapel added in 192 by the late Camille Pouliot, Judge of the Superior Cour who lived there and who was a descendant of the Genes family. Although shingled on the ends in the Frenc Canadian manner, the house is built of stone with wal

150

Manoir Mauvide-Genest at St-Jean
A seventeenth century seigneurie on the island of Orleans.

three feet thick. On these walls you can see the round dents made by cannon balls fired in the bombardment of 1759. Madame Pouliot smilingly referred to them as "the Admiral's visiting cards".

This lovely old manoir is on the outskirts of the village, facing a small park on the river. You are sure to see it, as the highway passes the door, but permission to go through the house must be obtained from Madame Pouliot.

St-François. Near the end of the island you will come to this small village. The present church of wood, plaster and stone was built in 1734, but the parish dates from about 1683.

From here the road turns inland and goes through lush farming country. We were disappointed to see that prosperity was causing the use of imitation brick. Tar-paper shingles were replacing the old clapboard and plaster on some of the farm buildings, and there was a network of telephone and electric light poles and wires leading to the houses, such as one sees in industrial towns and cities. However, nothing can really spoil the charm of this beautiful countryside. As we came to the river again we could look across and see the village and shrine of Ste-Anne-de-Beaupré on the mainland.

Ste-Famille, the oldest parish on the island, has one of the most picturesque churches, framed by characteristic Lombardy poplars. The church was begun in 1669 by Monseigneur de Laval, Bishop of Quebec, who had been granted the Seigneurie of Ile d'Orléans. The high altar and some of the **wooden statues** in the church were carved by the Levasseur brothers of Quebec, over two hundred years ago.

Many of the original settlers on the Island of Orleans

STE-FAMILLE

The oldest parish on the Island of Orleans.

came to Ste-Famille about three hundred years ago from the mainland villages of Beauport, L'Ange-Gardien and Château Richer to escape from the constant threat of attack by the Iroquois Indians. One of the pioneer houses, still standing, is known as the Robert Gagnon house, a substantial one-and-a-half story cottage of typical French Canadian design. Robert Gagnon settled in St-Famille as long ago as 1657.

Today, all around the village, you will see large orchards with modern farm houses, well painted and maintained, and as you approach the next settlement you will notice an increase in dairy farming, for this is the centre of the island's cheese industry.

St-Pierre. With the sole exception of the church, this entire parish was destroyed by fire during the war of 1759. The parish priest, who on that occasion gathered all the settlers and their crops within the walls of the old church, was later to become His Grace Bishop d'Esglis, the eighth bishop of Quebec. He continued, however, to live on the island among his old parishioners of St-Pierre.

A mile or so from this village you will come to the road leading to the bridge, and you will have completely circled the island. Those are the sights you will see on the way, and as you return to the mainland you will have a view of the Falls of Montmorency from the bridge.

We are sure you will find the island drive interesting and pleasant, but we hope you will stay on the Ile d'Orléans long enough to relax from the rush of the twentieth century tempo, for you will find rest there, and a certain tranquility for your mind and soul. Perhaps you may even find a new perspective on progress and the intrinsic values of life.

Part Four

SUMMER RESORTS AND SPECKLED TROUT

Chapter 10

THE LOWER ST. LAWRENCE
(NORTH SHORE)

ROAD LOG FOR HIGHWAY 15
From Quebec to Tadoussac and
on to Baie-Comeau

Miles

0	Quebec City
7	Montmorency Falls
21	Ste-Anne-de-Beaupré
62	Baie-St-Paul
73	Les Eboulements - Ile aux Coudres
91	La Malbaie (Murray Bay)
112	St-Siméon - Ferry to South Shore
137	Tadoussac - Saguenay River
261	Baie-Comeau - end of road

THIS ROUTE HAS EVERYTHING, except a good highway. Even that is being improved each year, so that there are now many miles of pavement, and the sights are exciting enough, and the resorts famous enough, to make the average motor tourist willing to ignore the bumps and the dust. Certainly, we would not miss visiting this Lower St. Lawrence, North Shore, for anything as trivial as a few miles of gravel.

The fast four lane Highway 15 follows the river from Quebec to Montmorency. The old road, known as 15A keeps to the upper level and goes through the ancient

Seigneurie of Beauport, which is not the same place as Lac-Beauport in the mountains. This region is often called the Beauport Shore and is one of the earliest French settlements, as it was part of the first seigneurie granted in Quebec.

Montmorency Falls. For those of you who like statistics perhaps we should tell you that **the falls are more than a hundred feet higher than Niagara,** having a drop of 274 feet. In summer an elevator will take you down to the foot of the falls if you want to see them at their best. To see them at their most impressive you should, of course, come in the spring time, or after heavy rains, when the river is in flood.

You may wonder what the pillars are doing on either side of the falls. They used to support a light suspension bridge. About a hundred years ago the bridge collapsed and carried a man and his wife over the falls to their deaths. Their bodies were not recovered, and a legend grew up that there was a subterranean passage under the bed of the St. Lawrence which never gave up its dead.

The villages in the vicinity of the falls are called St-Grégoire de Montmorency, St-Louis de Courville, and Boischâtel, but few people ever use those names. Montmorency is at the entrance to the bridge going to the Island of Orleans. Courville is at the forks of Highway 15. The Royal Quebec Golf Club is at Boischâtel, about two miles east of Kent House Hotel and the falls. The Royal Quebec has **a championship golf course,** 6525 yards long, and after your game you may have lunch, if you wish, in the dining room of the attractive club house.

L'Ange-Gardien is another ancient village. You will probably see a number of stalls along the way where

158

Canadian handicraft rugs, bedspreads and novelties are on sale. You will see, also, some of the loveliest of the Norman type of farm houses, many of them still using their outdoor bake ovens.

The new Highway 15 no longer goes through these delightful villages, which are strung along the old road in a haphazard and picturesque fashion, seldom more than a mile or two apart. If time is no object, they should certainly be seen.

Château Richer. If you have been wondering **what the old French Canadian farm houses look like on the inside,** here is your chance to find out. Baker's Inn, built as a farm about a hundred and seventy-five years ago, is still a farm, although it has opened its doors to visitors with a large dining room whose slogan is: *"You are Always on Time"*. We had a most satisfactory dinner there. The food was nicely cooked and served up, country style, in plentiful quantities for big appetites. This hospitable inn is only two-and-a-half miles from the world famous shrine of Ste-Anne-de-Beaupré.

Ste-Anne-de-Beaupré (Population 2,000). Hundreds of thousands of pilgrims, visitors and tourists throng to this town each year, so that its crowded main street gives the impression of being always *en fête*. The whole place is an amazing show, including museums, souvenir shops, guided tours, and an enormous Cyclorama of Jerusalem. To accommodate the great influx of people, a number of motels and motor courts have been built along the highway, within walking distance of the Shrine. The old, commercial type of hotels do a rushing business in the town.

Behind all this crowding and confusion lies something really beautiful, the story of Ste-Anne-de-Beaupré. A magnificent new Basilica has arisen on the traditional site of the first rude chapel, built in 1658 by grateful sailors to their patron Saint. Old documents tell of miracles that occurred while it was under construction, and during the three hundred years since then, although many chapels have been built, burned, and rebuilt, the miraculous statue of Saint Anne has been saved, and the miracles continue. Pilgrims come from all over the world, on crutches, in wheel chairs, or even carried on stretchers, to pray at Ste-Anne-de-Beaupré. It is one of the world's greatest manifestations of Faith. The new Basilica, which replaces the one burned in 1922, is now almost complete.

The chapel across the street commemorates the first stone church, erected in 1676, which remained in use for two hundred years. On the hill behind it are life-sized bronze figures depicting the Stations of the Cross, and the Scala Santa. The Côte de Beaupré belonged to the vast seigneuries of Bishop Laval, which included the Island of Orleans.

The census of 1667, according to Parkman, gives the population of the Beaupré seigneurie as 656, the Island of Orleans as 529, while 448 people were living in the settlement at Quebec. The entire white population of Canada was only 4,312, of which more than a quarter lived on the Laval seigneuries. About the time the first stone church was being built at Ste-Anne-de-Beaupré, Laval gave his seigneurie of Beaupré as an endowment to the Seminary of Quebec, which he had founded. Although he lived a life of austerity and poverty, Bishop Laval was the richest land-owner in the colony.

There is undoubtedly something exciting and inescapably impressive about Ste-Anne-de-Beaupré when the pilgrims are filling it to capacity and overflowing onto the

STE-ANNE-DE-BEAUPRÉ
The new Basilica is now almost complete.

hillside, but we like it best when it is quiet and still. Many people enjoy being part of a crowd. We feel that too many trippers spoil the scene. It is entirely a matter of preference, and you may take your choice. The crowded time is around the twenty-sixth of July, during the Festival of Saint Anne.

Beaupré. This village, about two miles from the Shrine, is the home of a pulp and paper mill. It is no longer a "beautiful meadow"—or, perhaps the place was named for the Vicomte de Beaupré, one of Jacques Cartier's companions in the ill-fated attempt to establish a colony at Cap-Rouge in 1541. The Ste-Anne River flows into the St. Lawrence at this point, and some of the loveliest old houses are here. One of them, standing in its own grounds a little back from the highway, has been transformed into **a small inn**.

From St-Joachim, site of the ancient Seminary of Quebec, the paved road runs inland from the river, through old villages and pleasant farms. Picturesque wooden bridges cross the streams. Near Baie-St-Paul the gravel road begins, which continues for most of the rest of the journey down the north side of the St. Lawrence.

Baie-St-Paul (Population 4,000). About two years ago this unpretentious small town attained nation-wide publicity when it was pictured by a prominent travel magazine as summing up the French Canadian way of life. Perhaps it does, insofar as one isolated spot can be typical of a huge area like Quebec. It nestles in the valley at the foot of a wooded mountain; its streets are narrow and winding; it has a big church on the main square, and a movie theatre that was playing a Laurel and Hardy comedy when we were there last year. Nearby, there is an interesting **old stone mill** and some charming stone farm houses that remain from the past. Unfortunately, the Baie-St-Paul Manor, built in 1718, was burnt down about 25 years ago. There are two small French Canadian hotels in the town, and you will find inns and boarding houses, some of which have over-night cabins, situated along the river and in the hills.

Forming a protective barrier across the wide mouth of the bay is the Ile aux Coudres, the island of the hazel-nut trees, so named by Jacques Cartier when he landed there more than four hundred years ago to plant a cross for France and to hear Mass, the first recorded Christian service held on Canadian soil. A ferry connects this rural island with the mainland.

Baie-St-Paul handicrafts have won high acclaim. The **wood carving of the Bouchards** rivals that of the famous school at St-Jean-Port-Joli, and **the hooked rugs depicting Quebec scenes designed and executed by Georges-Edouard Tremblay are works of art.** You will see them in the shops, and on the walls of many prominent buildings.

A road runs north to Grande-Baie on the Saguenay River, seventy-five miles away. It passes through St-Urbain and the scenes made famous by the Canadian artist, Clarence Gagnon.

You have a choice of roads going down the St. Lawrence. The inland highway 15A, is shorter, smoother and less hilly, but the old route that follows the river through Les Eboulements is more spectacular.

Les Eboulements. As its name tells you, there was once a landslide here. It happpened during the terrible earth-quake of 1663, when mountains covered with trees fell into the river and sank like pebbles. From Montreal to

Tadoussac the land was shaken. Eye-witness accounts describe the horrors: "a great roaring sound . . . the ground heaved . . . men and women seized with fright, knew not where to take refuge, expecting every moment to be buried under the ruins of the houses, or swallowed up in some abyss opening under their feet . . . a man ran all night to escape from a fissure in the earth which opened behind him as he fled."

All has been quiet here for almost three hundred years, but as you drive along you can still see the scars left by the earthquake.

A ferry runs from St-Joseph-de-la-Rive, near Les Eboulements, to Ile aux Coudres.

Murray Bay - La Malbaie (Population 1,500). It's old name of "The Bad Bay" is still used by the French Canadians, but the English re-named it in honour of General Murray, the first British Governor of Quebec.

This is one of Quebec's **most famous summer resorts**. It offers every type of accommodation, from the humblest guest house to the magnificent Manoir Richelieu, one of Canada's most palatial hotels.

The Manoir, owned by the Canada Steamship Lines, looks like a castle of the French Renaissance. It was named after Cardinal Richelieu, who played an important part in organizing the fur trade in Canada by heading the Hundred Associates of the Company of New France. King Louis XIII conferred on this company all the land from Florida to the Arctic Circle, forever, with a perpetual monopoly of the fur trade. The English, who discovered Hudson's Bay, and the Indians, who owned the land by right of possession, had something to say about that!

There is a handsome painting of Cardinal Richelieu

THE MANOIR RICHELIEU HOTEL
The show place of Murray Bay,

hanging in the hotel lobby. The lobby, in fact, is something of an art gallery, and the lounge has a most interesting collection of historical prints. We think you will find the whole building quite fascinating. The grounds are lovely, too, with an unusually fine swimming pool of heated salt water, good tennis courts, and one of the most interesting 18 hole golf courses in Quebec.

The Manoir is definitely the show place of Murray Bay, and it is something you should not miss. The rates are rather high. They have to be, to support such grandeur.

Some people think the Manoir is too big to be cosy, and many others feel they cannot afford it. For them we suggest one of the **small inns** on the main street of the village. Château Murray and Chamard's Lorne House, on the Pointe-au-Pic Road, have been popular for years. They are near the Murray Bay Golf Club and within easy walking distance of the many attractions at the Manoir Richelieu. There are also a number of **pensions** in and about the village. Many of the summer visitors have their own houses. Some people have been coming here for more than fifty years, which gives an air of permanency and selectivity to the social life of the colony.

The Manoir Richelieu has **a fishing lodge** in the nearby mountains, but there is not much fishing in the village. Murray Bay is primarily **a golfing resort**. As such we found it delightful, with two 18 hole courses. The climate was exhilarating and it was seldom too hot to enjoy the game.

There are very few villages after you leave Murray Bay and Cap-à-l'Aigle, but you will see an occasional habitant farm with an outdoor bake oven, and the rural scenery along the way is quite appealing.

St-Siméon (Population 1,000). **A ferry for passengers and cars** runs from here to Rivière-du-Loup, on the opposite side of the St. Lawrence. Meals are served on board. Many people use this ferry to avoid driving on gravel roads, as the highway on the south shore is paved. It makes several interesting circular trips possible, if you are spending the summer in this area.

A road runs north from St-Siméon, up the Saguenay to Lac St-Jean. We will be coming back in a little while to take this trip, but first we want you to see Tadoussac at the mouth of the Saguenay River, twenty-five miles farther on. It is something too lovely to miss.

The road is winding and there are many warnings: "Petite vitesse - Low gear."

You will also see signs: "Défense de pêcher - No fishing", because many of the small lakes are private property. We thought, at first, that this meant "No sinning". French accents have always bothered us.

A ferry runs every two hours across the mouth of the Saguenay River between Baie-Ste-Catherine and the ancient and historic village of Tadoussac.

Tadoussac. With the exception of Newfoundland, this is probably **the oldest trading post in Canada**, as even before the coming of Jacques Cartier, the Basque fishermen used this harbour to trade with the Indians.

The first settlement was attempted three hundred and fifty years ago when Pierre Chauvin, a naval captain, and Pontgravé, a merchant from Jacques Cartier's home town of St-Malo, landed here and built a cluster of wooden huts and a store-house. A fine reproduction of the store-house has been constructed on the original site, surrounded by a stout stockade, almost as if it were waiting for the Indians to come down the river to trade their furs. The Chauvin Post stands in the grounds of the new Tadoussac Hotel, and houses **an Indian museum**.

The Tadoussac Hotel, owned by the Canada Steamship Lines, was built in 1942. It replaces a resort that was fashionable in Victorian times, and many of the guests belong to the same families that came here before the turn of the century. It gives the place something the air of a smart club. In design, the French colonial idea has been faithfully carried out with pleasing results. It is a good place to come for a complete rest in a cool climate. For those who want some activity, there is a scenic and well-kept 9 hole golf course laid out in the hills, a short walk from the hotel.

Our bedroom was large and attractively furnished, and if we describe the view from our window it should give you a good idea of the place, as most of it can be seen at a glance.

To the left, just beyond the hotel grounds, we could see the Jesuit Mission Church of Saint Anne, built in 1747. A bell, brought from France in 1647, is all that remains of the former church, which was burnt. Once a year, on July 26th, the old bell is rung to celebrate the Festival of Saint Anne.

On the right, on a point of land projecting out into the river, one of the Canada Steamship Lines' cruise ships was unloading passengers. Instead of a taxi, a horse-drawn surrey was bringing guests up the winding road to the hotel. Two boats loaded with pulp wood were alongside the wharf. The hotel's cabin cruiser and several yachts were moored in the bay.

Nearby, some of the hotel guests were bowling on the green, others were playing the putting course, and a number of people were lounging in comfortable chairs, watching the scene.

TADOUSSAC
(*Above*) Jesuit Mission Church of Ste-Anne.
(*Below*) The Chauvin Store-house—the oldest trading post in Canada.

The rates, which include meals, were less than we expected to pay in such a smart hotel.

If you would rather live in a rustic setting, there is a nice **fishing camp** about seven miles from the village. It is a jolly place to swim, and there are lots of boats for fishing or rowing about the lake. It has private fishing waters, reserved for its guests, stocked with speckled trout and *ouananiche,* which are exciting to catch and mighty good to eat. The fishing camp is run by the Tadoussac Hotel, and the rates are a little lower.

Highway 15, a new and rather rough gravel road, passes the camp and continues as far as Baie-Comeau.

Baie-Comeau. We doubt if you will want to make this trip, unless you have business in this new, industrial town. The most comfortable way of getting to Baie-Comeau, until the roads have been improved, is to take the paved highway on the south shore of the St. Lawrence, and cross on the ferry from Rimouski.

One of the pleasant things to do while you are staying in Tadoussac, especially if you want a rest from driving, is to take **the famous Saguenay River cruise** up to Ha! Ha! Bay and back, which is as impressive and as awe inspiring as any river trip we have ever taken.

There is so much to see in that legendary land which the Indians and the early fur traders called "The Kingdom of the Saguenay" that we think it deserves a chapter all its own.

Chapter 11

UP THE SAGUENAY RIVER

THE SAGUENAY, with its magnificent scenery, is better seen from the river than from the road, but for those who have already taken the boat trip, this is an unusual route through the mountains, with occasional breathtaking glimpses of the deep, mysterious river.

Crossing on the ferry from Tadoussac to Baie-Ste-Catherine, one has a splendid view of the river. It was formed by glaciers cutting their course through the mountains at the end of the Great Ice Age. The deep dark waters and towering cliffs, with their unearthly echoes, caused the Indians to weave strange legends about the giant gods who lived there, and of the fabulous wealth to be found in the Kingdom of the Saguenay.

At present no road runs close to the river, although one is under construction on the Tadoussac side. The mountains, rising sharply to a height of almost two thousand feet, make road building difficult.

As you leave St-Siméon you follow the valley of the Rivière-Noire, along which there are a number of "Club de Pêche". These so-called fishing clubs, some of which are little more than shacks, often have fishing rights on a well-stocked lake or stream and offer good sport.

Presently you will be driving down the valley of the Petit-Saguenay which is like an artist's dream—strange pink colourings in the rocks—a log boom in a dammed up lake—a covered bridge over a mountain stream.

Petit-Saguenay is a straggling village which lies in the valley of the river of the same name. It has a few shops and a number of small houses which are strung for miles along the highway.

Anse-St-Jean. A road on the right goes to this settlement on the Saguenay River. It is off the highway, about ten minutes out of your way. Unless you are scenery blind you will be impressed by the majestic beauty all around Anse-St-Jean.

As you cross a fast running mountain stream that comes down from Lac Eternité, you will be approximately opposite the famous capes, but because of the precipitous and difficult terrain, there is no way at present of driving to see them.

There is a small settlement on Lac Otis, a narrow stretch of water that looks like a river, and thirteen miles beyond is Grande-Baie, where the hushed silences end and the busy crowded industrial towns begin.

Grande-Baie. You have come eighty miles by road from St-Siméon, but you are only sixty miles up the river. The deep inlet here is known as Ha! Ha! Bay. Its grim humour lies in the fact that Champlain, the first white man to explore the region, hoping to find the treasures described by the Indians and the long-sought route to China, wound up in the dead-end of this bay.

Chicoutimi (Population 30,000). It is almost impossible to keep pace with the rapid growth of this important industrial, agricultural and commercial centre which shares with its neighbours the advantages of hydro-electric power from Shipshaw. You will find modern stores and theatres along Rue Racine, and a handicraft shop selling **Saguenay homespuns** on Hy. 16. The prettiest route through the city is along the river road, Rue de la Rivière-du-Moulin.

From Chicoutimi the road follows the river upstream. On the opposite shore the banks are high and rocky, with patches of pink rock gleaming through the evergreens. On the summit a giant cross has been erected.

Arvida (Population 12,000). On the outskirts of the city you come to the enormous plant of the Aluminum Company of Canada. Its capacity, they told us, was two million pounds of aluminum ingots a day, and the area covered by the buildings was a mile and a half long by three-quarters of a mile wide. Nearby is **the model town** built by the company for its employees.

There is something fantastic about this beautiful city that sprang, full-fledged, from the architect's drafting boards. Each house stands in its own spacious grounds. There are no slums. The parks and recreational centres were laid out as part of the original plan.

One of the most attractive of the public buildings is the Saguenay Inn, built of stone in the architecture of old Brittany. The interior is artistically furnished and pleased us in every way. We are sure you will enjoy staying overnight or longer in this charming setting. Rates are reasonable.

For amusement, there are flood-lighted **tennis courts, and a 9 hole golf course**. For sights to see there is **the spectacular hydro-electric power development** just a few miles up the river at Shipshaw, with a capacity of one million five hundred thousand horsepower, most of which is supplied to the Aluminum Company. It is as picturesque an industrial development as we have seen for many a day.

Another site you might like to look at is the new Aluminum Bridge over the Saguenay, completed in 1950. It connects the city with a park on the opposite side, and is a short route to the No. 2 Shipshaw Power House.

Adjoining Arvida there is a well settled and fairly old farming district, the beginning of the northern clay belt.

Kénogami and Jonquière (Population 25,000). As they are only a mile apart and are rapidly growing together, these two places already appear to be one and the same. At Kénogami there is a fine view of the Shipshaw dams from the top of the hill. A bridge crosses at low level to the opposite shore. Jonquière is a new and fast growing city, with every facility to serve the vast farming area around it. Highway 16 runs through the main street where the town maintains an information bureau for tourists.

After the spectacular mountain scenery and the wildness of the river gorge, it is amazing to find oneself in flat farming country. There are farms in all directions, as far as the eye can see, to the parish of St-Bruno where Highway 16 ends.

St-Joseph-D'Alma (Population 10,000). Another new

(*Above*) The Saguenay Inn, Arvida, is Built in the Architecture of Old Brittany (*Below*) A Fishing Camp Near Tadoussac

town that is fast growing into a city, St-Joseph-d'Alma is situated at a strategic position where the Saguenay River flows out of Lac St-Jean. The first big power house on the Saguenay was built at nearby Ile Maligne twenty-five years ago, and the industrial boom began.

Just as abruptly as we entered a highly developed modern community, we leave it again for the peaceful isolation of farming and lumbering and for the thrills of **some of the finest fishing in Quebec**. We have arrived at Lac St-Jean, the home of Louis Hémon's famous heroine, Maria Chapdelaine.

Chapter 12

AROUND LAKE ST. JOHN

EVERYONE WHO HAS READ *Maria Chapdelaine*, and many who have not, will be anxious to take the unusual one-hundred-and-fifty mile drive around Lac St-Jean. **About a third of the route has been paved**, mostly along the south shore. The rest is gravel, but it takes you to **some wonderful fishing and hunting territory**, and once there you will travel mostly in boats and canoes.

Ile Maligne. Leaving St-Joseph-d'Alma behind you and travelling north and westward, you will cross the two branches of the Saguenay, known as the Little Discharge and the Big Discharge, and on the Ile Maligne you will see the half million horsepower plant where the taming of the tempestuous Saguenay River began. This was lumbering country long before the advent of electric power, and it still is. Here and at many other places along the route there are large pulp and paper mills.

After the lumbering came the pioneer farms, and you will see many of them as you drive along. At Honfleur, where the highway crosses the Péribonca River, you will be tempted, as we were, to look for the settler's cabin where Maria Chapdelaine lived with her family, "on the other side of the river above the falls, more than a dozen miles away" from Péribonca.

Péribonca. In the book, it is spelled with a K. The Quebec maps use the C. You may take your choice. In this small settlement you will find more concrete evidence of the impact which Maria Chapdelaine has made on its readers. Here, where the story began, is the **Musée Louis Hémon**, a museum planned to be a permanent memorial to the author of the "Tale of Lake St. John". Many of you will want to linger here, to reconstruct for yourselves the scenes of the story, for although the book was written almost forty years ago, life has not changed so very much in this outpost of civilization.

Mistassini. This, you will remember, was the home of François Paradis, the ill-fated hero of the book. There before you lies **the old Trappist monastery** "squatting between the river and the heights". You will have no difficulty finding a wooden bridge "covered in and painted red, not unlike an amazingly long Noah's Ark", for many of the bridges, all over the Province of Quebec, still cling to this old design.

This is **blueberry country**. Have you ever seen the rocks and fields for miles around covered with these modest little plants in bloom? Too small to be showy, they appeal to us for the helpful and useful way they

LAKE ST. JOHN COUNTRY

(Above) The open lake, so wide it appeared to be boundless.
(Below) Hydro-electric power development at Shipshaw on the Saguenay.

cover up the ravages of a sweeping forest fire. If the berries are ripe we know you will enjoy a juicy deep blueberry pie.

Dolbeau (Population 3,000) is a model pulp and paper town, company planned, with **a small inn** which can offer you a room with a private bath—rather unusual in this remote corner of Quebec. The River of the Rats, which here flows into the wide Mistassini River, is named for the fur-bearing muskrat, and not for the unpleasant city type of rodent.

Albanel. Small places sometimes commemorate great deeds, and this tiny settlement on the edge of nowhere is named in honour of the Jesuit Father Charles Albanel, who in the days of Count Frontenac, and under the auspices of the Intendant Talon, made a remarkable voyage of discovery from Tadoussac, up the Saguenay River and through Lac St-Jean, to Hudson's Bay.

Normandin (Population 3,000). Typical of the farming communities which strangely enough predominate in this Lac St-Jean country, Normandin is a prosperous centre, with **sawmills, cheese factories**, and the usual stores. It is the farthest extension westward of the travelled highway, although a few roads, which may some day develop into highways, do penetrate the bush beyond, notably in the area of the government's new fishing reserve of Chibougamau.

St-Félicien (Population 4,000). Although this thriving agricultural town has a year-round existence in its own right as a centre for dairying and market-gardening, it is probably destined to become known as "The Gateway to the **Chibougamau Fishing Reserve**". The fisherman who will go any distance to angle in virgin waters will be in his element here. A bush road leads westward through this new Provincial Park. It is desirable to carry a tent and supplies along, as at present few accommodations are provided in the reserve. Guides are available, and supplies may be purchased at St-Félicien. Fly fishing, casting, spinning and trolling are allowed.

In the rivers and lakes of this area you will find speckled trout, lake trout, *ouananiche,* pickerel (*doré*) and northern pike. As in all Quebec Provincial Parks, no hunting is allowed.

St-Prime. This charming old parish belongs to the legend of Maria Chapdelaine. When the book begins, Maria had been visiting her mother's relations in this small settlement on the lake. An almost pathetic touch is her father's remark: "She has had plenty of gaiety at St-Prime."

Roberval (Population 4,000). The sportsman will be in his element here, for although Roberval is a town of considerable importance as a shopping centre, it is even more important as the jumping off place for about **the best hunting and fishing to be had in this corner of Quebec**.

The serious hunter or fisherman, who wants to go where the sport is best, should get in touch with Léonce Hamel & Son, of Roberval. They have leased from the Quebec Government the sole hunting and fishing rights to several hundred square miles in the Lac St-Jean area. They will arrange everything for you, and will supply all equipment, including French Canadian guides, canoes, lodging and provisions. Rates are high, but they always are, everywhere, for this kind of sport. The hunting season for moose and deer begins the middle of September and lasts a month. Duck and goose shooting is from the first of September until the end of October.

If you do not want to make an expedition of it, or if the cost is beyond you, why not try your luck fishing for *ouananiche*, the famous land-locked salmon of Lac St-Jean? You can arrange that quite reasonably, through the Château Roberval Hotel. The season for *ouananiche* is from the first of May to September thirtieth, but the best fishing is usually late in the summer.

St-Jérôme (Population 3,000). As we stood on the high bluffs, although the day was clear, we searched in vain for a glimpse of the opposite shore as we looked out across the open lake, so wide it appeared to be boundless. Actually it is about twenty-five miles long by twenty miles wide. Around us, as far as we could see in all directions looking landward, there was nothing but farms. Fine crops of oats and barley, cattle grazing, big barns and modern chicken houses, a flat and green terrain. The hills in the distance seemed very far away.

A few miles up the shore we could see the farms of St-Gédéon, the fictional home of Maria Chapdelaine's mother.

Hébertville (Population 1,500). About six miles inland from the lake, Hébertville is the junction point for the highways. The road on the left, going north, will take you back to St-Bruno and St-Joseph-d'Alma. The road on the right, going south, is Highway 54A leading to one of Quebec's **most famous fishing reserves**. Here you will find that rare combination—good fly fishing for speckled trout—good accommodations in well run camps —and good highways to take you there—three very good reasons why you will not want to miss Le Parc des Laurentides.

Chapter 13
THROUGH LAURENTIDE PARK

ROAD LOG FOR HIGHWAY 54A AND 54
Going south through the Park

Miles

Miles	
0	Hébertville - Lac St-Jean
9	Northern Entrance to Park
25	Le Gîte Fishing Camp
64	Junction with Highway 54B from Chicoutimi
70	Jacques Cartier Fishing Camp
72	Le Relais Inn
103	Southern Entrance to Park
136	The City of Quebec

ROAD LOG FOR HIGHWAY 54 AND 54B
Going north through the Park

Miles	
0	Quebec
33	Southern entrance to Park
64	Le Relais Inn
66	Jacques Cartier Camp
72	Junction with Highway 54A from Lac St-Jean
136	Chicoutimi

THE LAURENTIDE PARK, or Le Parc des Laurentides, is a fishing reserve of more than four thousand square miles of lakes, rivers and streams, flowing through wild forest and bush country and connected with Quebec, Chicoutimi and Lac St-Jean by fine new paved highways. Another road, Highway 56, runs north from Baie-St-Paul to Ha! Ha! Bay, skirting the eastern edges of the park on its way.

This is the place to come for a fishing holiday. It will delight the fly fishing enthusiast, as no other bait or tackle is allowed in the reserve. This is the native habitat of the speckled trout (*truite mouchetée*) and when we were there, during the first two weeks in July, he was rising beautifully to a Dark Montreal and to a Brown Hackle. Our friends in the next fishing camp were having good luck with a Royal Coachman—but the fly varies with the weather and the season and no rules can be laid down for such a subtle and changeable thing as the whim of a speckled trout.

In only one lake is there any other kind of fishing. Jacques Cartier, one of the largest of the park's 1,500 lakes, has rainbow and grey trout, but here as elsewhere fly-fishing only is the rule.

We spent so much time climbing mountains and hiking along the forest trails, hunting wild life with our cameras, that our fishing was reduced to a minimum, but we saw and sampled the many fine catches made by our friends who, like true fishermen, were up at dawn and away with a guide to fish the nearby rivers and streams. Sometimes, if their luck was good, they did not return to camp but spent the night at one of the **cabin shelters** which are scattered through the park for just such a contingency.

Even if you do not want to fish, or to hunt with a camera, you will be certain to enjoy the highways—wide and smooth with no crossroads and very little traffic. The speed limit is 60 miles an hour.

If you are just driving through, you may get a free travel permit at either of the gates, but if you intend to fish, that is another matter. You should **apply to the Park Superintendent for a fishing permit and for reservations**. His address is: Department of Game and Fisheries, Room 116, Block E, Parliament Buildings, Quebec. While you are in the city of Quebec, you can ask about it at the Provincial Tourist Bureau, 106 Grande-Allée, and they will give you the necessary information.

Some of the camps are run like small resort inns, while others are for rent furnished, with boats but without service, and are suitable for fishing clubs or for parties of fishermen to rent by the week, month or season.

But enough of generalities. Suppose we take you with us through the park and let you see for yourself what it is like.

When we left Lake St. John, we turned south on Highway 54A and headed for the Laurentide Park. The farming country was behind us, and soon we were back in the woods again, with great outcroppings of pink granite all around us.

Parc des Laurentides. At the entrance there is a barrier and a post of the Dept. of Lands and Forests. If you have not already obtained a travel permit in Quebec, they will give you one here. This is a precaution against forest fires, and also against people fishing these waters who have no right to do so.

The most northerly of the fishing camps is near the barrier, on Lac de la Belle-Rivière, one of the larger lakes. The Belle-Rivière Lodge can accommodate ten fishermen, and the right to fish in this area belongs to the guests at the Lodge.

As soon as you cross the covered bridge over the wide

and fast running Rivière-aux-Écorces you are out of the Belle-Rivière reserve and into the waters that belong to the guests of Le Gîte Camp, seven and a half miles away. If you stay at Le Gîte, you may fish all the lakes, rivers and streams in this area. Some of the lakes can be reached only by trails through the woods, but you will find canoes waiting for you when you get there. Some of the more remote rivers have sleeping cabins, which you use if you do not wish to return to camp. Twenty miles westward, off the "beaten track", there are two camps on Lac aux Écorces, where you may go with a guide.

Le Gîte, with eight cottages, is on pretty Lac Clarence-Gagnon, named after the distinguished Quebec painter. If there are four or less in your party, it is a good place to stay. You may rent a small cabin by the day, with two or three rooms, a fireplace or stove, and a wash room. The cottages are built of logs, painted yellow, and all the guests meet in the comfortable main lodge for meals. You may swim at your door from the beach or diving tower. Row boats are always available for fishing the small lake, but you will probably have better luck if you fish the rivers and streams some distance away from the highway. The steward, who is also bartender and information bureau, will tell you where to go and how to get there, if you prefer to fish without a guide.

Le Gîte means a lodging or shelter, but we found it was much more than that. The meals were far better than we expected in the north woods, and they were served with considerable style by the steward and his wife.

La Passe is a small camp about eight miles down the

LAURENTIDE PARK
(Top) Le Gîte Fishing Camp. *(Middle)* You may see a family of bears.
(Bottom) The Montmorency River at Mares du Sault.

highway. Beyond it you will see no human habitation for some distance, but you may see a deer or a family of bears.

At the Grand-Pikauba River there is **a large camp with five lodges**, some of which can accommodate eight people. We did not find out where the Lodge got its rather startling name of **Portes de l'Enfer**—the Gates of Hell.

Nearby, at a fork in the road, the two routes from the north join each other. Highway 54B from Chicoutimi is a fast new road, but at present there are no camps along it. It traverses long stretches of rather swampy land, covered with stunted hemlock, spruce and tamarack trees. The blue hush of the distant hills is awe-inspiring, and the lakes and rivers lost in this vastness are **teeming with trout**. They can be fished best from canoes.

Jacques Cartier Lake. Probably the largest concentration of camps to be found in the park is here, not far from the junction of the two roads. It could hardly be called a settlement, but there is a service station, a number of cottages and camps along the shores of the lake, and the Auberge L'Étape, the only inn that stays open all year. It welcomes motorists who are just passing through, but Jacques Cartier is a good lake for the fisherman, too. There are rainbow and grey trout, as well as speckled trout, and we saw some fine catches taken from these waters while we were there.

Le Relais is another camp for the motorist, and for the casual fisherman. The pretty little lake, at an elevation of 2,652 feet, is called Horatio Walker, after the well-known painter of Quebec scenes. The dining room at Le Relais is open to the passer-by, and there are ten small cottages in connection with the inn that may be rented by the day.

Also in this area are the two camps known as Bouleaux Lodge and Camp Sept-Iles. Each will accommodate four people, and each has good fishing waters at its disposal.

Mares du Sault. Fish were jumping all around us at this scenic spot on the Montmorency River, the same river that tumbles over the escarpment near the Kent House to form Montmorency Falls. There is a camping ground for tents and trailers here, and you may fish the river with a one day licence.

The highway reaches its highest elevation at Des Roches Hill, which is 2,868 feet above sea level. You will not be particularly conscious of being in the mountains, however, because the whole plateau is high and the peaks are not spectacular, but you can feel it in the exhilarating air.

At the southern barrier a park attendant will stop you, and, in case you do not understand his French, he will be asking you to surrender your Laurentide Park travel permit.

On the way back to Quebec, at the village of **Notre-Dame-des-Laurentides**, you will pass the road going in to Lac Beauport and the popular Manoir St-Castin Hotel. A little farther on you may turn off at Charlesbourg, and, if you have not seen enough wild animals in the park, you may see them here, in the zoo.

Near **Charlesbourg** you will find the ruins of the Château of Beaumanoir, where the dastardly Intendant Bigot once lived with his captive Indian girl, Caroline de St. Castin. In *The Golden Dog* Kirby described the Château as "a long, heavy structure of stone, gabled and pointed in the style of the preceding century—strong enough for defence, and elegant enough for the abode of the Royal Intendant of New France."

There are **several park establishments not on the highways,** which we think you might like to know about. For example, the camps along the Metabetchouan River

Perhaps **the most attractive camp of all** is Sainte-Anne Lodge, built on an island in Lac Ste-Anne, reached by Highway 56. It was formerly a private hunting and fishing lodge, but now it may be rented, complete with service, by a family or group of fishermen. It can accommodate up to twelve people, and it has the exclusive rights to many square miles of fishing territory. It is the next best thing to owning your own fishing camp.

The rates vary greatly, according to the type of cabin you occupy and the waters you fish, but if it is speckled trout you are looking for, we can think of no place that offers you a wider choice of accommodations for a fly fishing holiday than Le Parc des Laurentides.

The time has come now for us to leave the North Shore and to travel down to the sea along the South Shore of the St. Lawrence River.

There will be some among you who are looking forward with keen anticipation to catching an Atlantic salmon in the Matapédia, the Cascapédia, or one of the other salmon rivers that flow into the Baie des Chaleurs. For some the lure will be the scenery of Percé, or, perhaps, the bird sanctuary on Bonaventure Island.

Whatever the goal, the trip around the Gaspé is the most celebrated motor tour in Quebec, a spectacular blending of seacoast, sea gulls and scenery.

Part Five

THE WORLD FAMOUS GASPÉ TOUR

Chapter 14

THE LOWER ST. LAWRENCE
(SOUTH SHORE)

ROAD LOG FOR HIGHWAYS 2 AND 10
From Lévis to Ste-Flavie

Miles

0	Quebec - Lévis
35	Montmagny
58	St-Jean-Port-Joli
75	Ste-Anne-de-la-Pocatière
92	Kamouraska
114	Notre-Dame-du-Portage
120	Rivière-du-Loup - Hy. 2 goes to New Brunswick. Follow Hy. 10
124	Cacouna
146	Trois-Pistoles
175	Bic
187	Rimouski - Pointe-au-Père
203	Ste-Flavie - Mont-Joli. Start of the circular tour of Gaspé

WHEN THE HUGE QUEBEC BRIDGE was built in 1917 it was hailed as one of the wonders of the world. The river, at this point, had defied man's engineering skill for years. The first attempt, begun in 1907, ended in disaster when the half-completed structure collapsed.

The second attempt, begun in 1916, was also marked for tragedy. The centre span, 640 feet long, crashed into

193

the river while it was being hoisted into place, carrying several men to their deaths. Finally, about a year later, the bridge was successfully completed.

People came from near and far to see it, but they could not drive across it, as it had been designed for railway trains only. We walked out on it at night and it seemed almost human, the way it swayed and groaned.

Twelve years after the opening of the bridge, the same year that the spectacular road around Gaspé was completed, a vehicular lane was added, but this soon became obsolete. We were glad to see, when we drove across the Quebec Bridge last summer, that workmen were busy widening the road and building new approaches. This year it should be a fine fast route to the South Shore, and it is still **a marvel of engineering skill well worth seeing**.

The Lévis ferries run every twenty minutes and save about fifteen miles of driving, but we think it would be a great pity to miss seeing the Quebec Bridge.

Sometimes we flip a coin for it. Heads the ferry— tails the bridge. We always feel disappointed when it comes up heads.

Lévis (Population 14,000). The nicest thing about Lévis is its views. Champlain named the point Cap Lévy. The city was called Lévis in honour of the hero of the battle of Ste-Foy. We do not want to disparage this pleasant place, but after Quebec it does seem a bit dull. The comparison will always be inevitable. Historic sites are few. The "Fortifications" are less than a hundred years old. However, the skyline of Quebec across the river is most impressive; **the falls of the Chaudière River**, nearby, are quite attractive; there is **a golf course**; and there is a really fine vantage point, a short distance down the river, from which to view the Montmorency Falls. As we drove along we could see the celebrated *Chute*, beyond the Island of Orleans, and we thought it looked much wider and more beautiful against its background of mountains than it did at close range.

Lauzon (Population 8,000) is really a continuation of the city of Lévis. Lauzon is best known for its **enormous drydocks**. The Champlain Drydock is one of the largest in the world.

The first time we drove over this route was more than twenty years ago. The last time was a few months ago. Happily there have not been too many changes. We always find the scenery spectacular and the towns and villages interesting.

On a bright day, especially if there are white clouds in a blue sky, you will get the illusion of lovely paintings being opened before you at every turn, each more beautiful than the last.

Beaumont. The old seigneurie of Vincennes was here, granted in the year 1672 by the Intendant Talon to a François Bissot, with three miles frontage on the river.

A mill was built in 1733 by Claude-Joseph Roy, who later bought the seigneurial manor of Vincennes. His daughter became involved in a scandal with the infamous Intendant Bigot, villain of *The Golden Dog*. Her indiscretions gave the Vincennes Mill the name of *Friponne*— the cheat.

Many of the houses belonging to the French regime are still standing. Probably the most interesting of the old buildings is the church, completed in 1733, and still very much in use. People are always looking for "typical" French Canadian settlements. Beaumont seems to us to be a "typical" and charming eighteenth century village.

St-Michel (Population 1,000), lying between the farm lands and the river, is turning into something of a small summer resort, with several auberges and overnight cabins. The new road, part of the Trans-Canada Highway, goes behind St-Michel and the villages of **St-Vallier**, called after the second Bishop of Quebec, and **Berthier**. The old, narrow road still runs through the centre of these settlements, if you want to look at their ancient manor houses.

Montmagny (Population 6,000). The highway runs the length of Rue St-Jean-Baptiste, the main shopping street, where you will find movie theatres, shops and garages. Montmagny was named after the Governor of New France who succeeded Frontenac and who laid out the Governor's Garden at the Château in Quebec. This is the largest town for some miles around. The Montmagny Inn, at the bridge near the centre of town, has been **a popular commercial hotel** for many years. It has a nice location beside a small river, with ample space for parking, which makes it a convenient stop.

In cold or rainy weather, we sometimes choose a small town for an over-night stop in preference to the seashore. On these occasions we try to see a Paris-made movie. We think it is a good way to polish our very rusty French.

Cap-St-Ignace. A few miles along the route you will come to the village of Cap-St-Ignace, with its fine stone church around which the small houses cluster in a characteristically French Canadian fashion. The Parish Hall and the Manoir are more than two hundred years old.

The wharf appears, at low tide, to be built in a meadow, beyond which there are islands in the river, set against an impressive back-drop of mountains on the North Shore.

L'Islet, the next village, has a Chambre du Commerce, which bids "Bienvenue aux Touristes". **The town has some interesting old houses** of the *habitant* style, an eighteenth century church, and a few unpretentious auberges, pensions and inns.

You may have the urge to stay in one of these small, French Canadian hotels, to get away from other English-speaking sight-seers. When we feel that way, we usually plan on stopping at St-Jean-Port-Joli, **the home of Quebec's renowned wood carvers**.

St-Jean-Port-Joli (Population 1,000). On the outskirts of the village, you will pass **the old bake-house**, or Vieux Four, which belonged to the Aubert de Gaspé Manor. It was here that Philippe Aubert de Gaspé, seigneur and author, wrote *Les Anciens Canadiens* which has saved for us so many reminiscences of bygone days.

The first wood carver's shop stands beside the Vieux Four. Here you may buy miniature boats, and beautifully carved figures, the work of Jean and André Bourgault, Eugène Leclerc, Paul Caron, and many others. There are several shops in the village where this unusual handicraft is displayed and sold.

The Bourgault brothers rank high among Quebec's skilled wood sculptors. Much of their work is of a religious nature, and very fine. They are largely responsible for the successful school of wood carvers at St-Jean-Port-Joli. There are other handicrafts, too, but this is predominantly the wood carvers' village.

There is a large modern auberge on the highway which gets a good deal of the tourist traffic passing through on the way to the Gaspé. However, our stopping place is the humble **village inn**, the Castel-des-Falaises—as truly French Canadian as any we have visited. It is back from the road, beyond the church. Each time we have been there, we were the only English-speaking people in the place. For an over-night stop, we like the cottage on the Falaise—a beautiful wooded cliff above the St. Lawrence. This cottage has private bathrooms, a sitting room, and a fine view. It is far above the standard of the rooms in the hotel. The meals are good farm style, and about the best in town.

The church on the main square dates from 1779, and is one of the few built in the Quebec *habitant* design, with no attempt to be Gothic or grand. We think it is particularly pleasing.

This is an "atmosphere" stopping place. There is nothing smart or fashionable about it, but we think you will enjoy it, especially if you are interested in Quebec handicrafts.

St-Roch-des-Aulnets, a few miles farther on, is a farming and milling village where Arthur Dubé, another sculptor in wood, has his studio and shop. An iron cross by the roadside is dated 1715, and near it there are **several old stone houses, over two hundred years old**, with the well-balanced, low-sweeping roof lines that artists love to paint.

Rocky hummocks and hills begin to rise abruptly from the level fields, like miniature mountain ranges, covered with evergreens. Across the St. Lawrence lies Ile aux Coudres, behind which the Laurentians roll away into the distant sky, casting lovely shadows of purple and blue all around them.

Ste-Anne-de-la-Pocatière (Population 5,000). The high road goes through this town, which is an educational and agricultural centre. The large buildings on the heights belong to the Classical College, to the Agricultural High School, and to the Fisheries High School. There is, also, an experimental farm. The Hotel St-Louis on the busy, crowded main street, is a neat and clean commercial hotel.

It is not necessary to go through this town, as the low road, which keeps close to the sea, is wider, smoother and shorter.

Rivière-Ouelle. The river makes a harbour for small boats. The village is rural, with some old farm houses and barns. Presently a high and rocky ridge shuts off the St. Lawrence to the north, and the road runs through a flat and fertile valley between the hills.

Near **St-Denis** you will see **typical Quebec farms**, with buildings of early colonial architecture, and with long narrow fields fenced in by split rails.

Kamouraska. Across the St. Lawrence, on a clear day, you can see the Manoir Richelieu at Murray Bay. In the middle of the river there are islands, with a lighthouse marking the channel for the ocean liners going up to Quebec and Montreal.

Kamouraska was the religious and civil centre for the Lower St. Lawrence east of Rivière-Ouelle from 1692 until 1791, according to the Commission des Monuments Historiques. Memorial crosses have been erected in the fields where once stood a church and *presbytère*. In the old cemetery one thousand three hundred pioneers are buried, near where the first church was built, in 1709.

The present village has a tidal wharf, and a yellow brick church built in 1914. Only a few of the ancient houses remain.

At **Andréville**, a pretty village set in the midst of odd

rocky ridges, the high road and the low road meet and continue together as one.

Notre-Dame-du-Portage is a gay and colourful **seaside resort**, particularly popular with French Canadians. The road runs so close to the water's edge that it appears to be crowding the hotels and cottages into the sea. Small resorts, inns, cabins and cottages border the highway. The tennis courts always seem to be in play, whenever we pass, and the "No Vacancy" signs are usually up at most of the overnight stopping places.

The portage was a road built by Governor Haldimand in 1783 to avoid the long sea voyage around the Gaspé Peninsula.

St. Patrick will be called **St-Patrice** on your map, but most of the summer residents, who have been coming here for several generations, use the English name. This small and fashionable resort is unusual in that it has no smart hotel, and very little accommodation of any kind for the traveller.

Chouinard's, an unassuming **guest house**, has been going for about fifty·years and is always filled with people who come back, summer after summer. Even if there were a vacancy, one feels that it would be very bad form to go to Chouinard's for the first time.

A short distance east of the golf club, is the summer home of Prime Minister Louis St. Laurent. Another Prime Minister, Sir John A. Macdonald, used to spend his summers at St. Patrick, from 1873 to 1890.

It is an altogether charming and delightful place, but we hesitate to recommend it. The casual passer-by, who has no friends living there, might feel rather left out of things.

(*Top*) The Summer Home of Prime Minister Louis St. Laurent
at St. Patrick   (*Middle*) Rivière-du-Loup
(*Bottom*) Cascade Hotel at Metis

Rivière-du-Loup (Population 10,000). The river of the Wolf has been harnessed for power, but the waterfall is still pretty in flood time. The city is important as the principal shopping centre for a large farming area. It began its existence in 1680, when the outlaw *coureurs des bois* had a large storehouse on the Rivière-du-Loup. It was filled with goods to trade with the Indians, in contempt of the King's orders, and much to the displeasure of the Governor, Count Frontenac.

Under the name of Fraserville, this part of the old Fraser seigneurie became a town. About that time, the Hotel Le Manoir was built on Rue de la Cour, near the church. **The hotel** has been very well maintained, and today it makes a pleasant over-night stop. We like its long verandahs, and there is a nice view from the sun porches in the rear. The dining room has a Victorian dignity and satisfactory food, and many of the bedrooms have private baths.

Another suitable over-night stop, for those who prefer towns to seaside villages, is the St. Louis Inn, **a commercial hotel** at the top of the hill on the main street, (Hy. 2). This is the road to New Brunswick. If you are taking the Gaspé trip, follow Highway 10 out of town.

A ferry runs three times a day between Rivière-du-Loup and St-Siméon, on the north shore of the St. Lawrence.

Cacouna, like St. Patrick, has been a fashionable summer resort for a great many years. The private summer cottages are impressive, each in its own well-kept garden. There is **a handicraft shop** in the village, tennis courts, and a few cabins for over-night guests. Nearby there are fine and prosperous farms. A network of secondary

oads runs for many miles inland from the St. Lawrence
through the farming area.

Ile-Verte is not only an island, it is also **a picturesque
village**, with a *filature*—a spinning mill—beside a waterfall.

Hay-making is still done in the old-fashioned way—
pitched by hand and hauled by horse. Tractors are a
rarity in this rural community, which follows the *habitant*
pattern. English is seldom heard.

Ile aux Basques. A few miles farther on we crossed the
Rivière-des-Trois-Pistoles. On the nearby Ile aux Basques,
in the St. Lawrence, the Provancher Society has established a bird sanctuary.

There is every reason to believe that Basques were
fishing in the Gulf of St. Lawrence in the fifteenth
century, before the coming of Cabot or Columbus. They
were trading with the Indians of the Saguenay, just
across the river from Ile aux Basques, in the sixteenth
century. As their interest was almost entirely in fishing,
and not in colonizing, they have been given little credit
for their discoveries in North America. They are remembered in the name of this small island, and perhaps
the bird sanctuary will revive an interest in these almost
forgotten early explorers.

Trois-Pistoles (Population 2,500) has stone quarries,
lumber mills, a large post office and a huge church. **A
Ferry** for passengers runs from the small but busy harbour
to **Les Escoumains** on the north shore, near **Tadoussac**.

The road goes through **St-Simon**, a farm village with
typical long and narrow fields. At the next village of
St-Fabien there is a peat bog, where the turf was being
cut and dried for export.

And now the odd rock formations of Bic begin—jagged hills and high hummocks, and unusually lovely views.

Bic (Population 3,000). There is no other place quite like Bic, and if you see it for the first time at sunset, it may grip your imagination, as it did ours, and you will not be able to go on until you have explored its brooding Massacre Island, and its strange miniature mountains which, according to the legends, were dropped from the apron of an angel.

There is nothing much here of reality. It is a place of mood. You must be able to see pictures in the odd little mountains and in the flat, stony surface of the sea bed when the tide has gone out leaving the islands high and dry, like stranded ships.

This is another "atmosphere" stop—recommended with reservations. It is for the artist—not for the "bon vivant".

L'Auberge du Français, just west of the town, has **over-night cabins** and rooms in the hotel. It is all very French. The dining room serves regular meals, or they will pack a picnic lunch for you, if you wish. The Bic **Golf Club**, on a point of land beyond the village, has a 9 hole course in a scenic setting. You can swim at Bic, but only at high tide.

After leaving Bic, you will pass through **Sacré-Coeur**, a rural village with a small summer settlement on the river, and then you will arrive at the scene of the horrible fire of 1950.

Rimouski (Population 10,000). During the ten years preceding the fire, Rimouski had grown in size and importance. It was a busy, progressive, industrial city when we were there in 1949. When we drove through it, shortly after the awful devastation, we wondered if it could ever rise again.

Rebuilding had already begun, but black ruin was everywhere and the sickening smell that follows in the wake of fire was hanging in the air. There was nothing left along Rue St-Germain in the centre of the city, where once the principal hotels, shops and movies had been. Black, stark remnants of trees still stood to mark the site of houses and gardens. It was all so sad that we could not bear to linger, but time will undoubtedly heal the scars.

East of the town, at the port of Rimouski, the steamships of the Lower St. Lawrence Transportation Company were at the big wharves, ready to leave on **cruises down the river** to Clarke City and Seven Islands. **A ferry** for cars and passengers runs to **Baie-Comeau** on the north shore.

Pointe-au-Père. Off the tall light house on the point is where ocean steamships stop to pick up river pilots for the trip up the St. Lawrence, and to drop them off again on the return voyage.

This was the scene of a marine disaster in 1914, when the *Empress of Ireland* sank with heavy loss of life. You will see the monument to the victims near the village, as you drive along.

Ste-Luce. An interesting old stone house beside the sea has been turned into **a tourist information bureau** and antique shop. We thought the cottages called Au Bec Fin, at Ste-Luce-sur-Mer, were particularly suitable for people travelling with children, as there is a pleasant sandy beach at the door. A lunch counter and dining room are run in connection with the cottages.

From Ste-Luce to where the Gaspé road begins, nine

miles away, the highway runs close to the boulder-strewn shore. The St. Lawrence is so wide at this point that you can no longer see across it. We noticed that fishing weirs and traps were more in evidence, and that the farms were decreasing in size and number as the smell of salt grew stronger.

It is always a question in people's minds as to where the river ends and the ocean begins. Some say it is where the tide starts. Others claim that it is a matter of the freshness of the water. Still others say it is where the river pilots take over the ships from the sea-going captains.

Wherever it may be, by the time you reach **St-Flavie** and the Gaspé road there can be no doubt about it—you have come down to the sea.

Po1Pose1

Chapter 15

THE GASPÉ ROAD

WHEN WE FIRST DROVE AROUND the Gaspé Peninsula, the year after the opening of the road, it was a somewhat hazardous expedition. The trail was narrow, winding and extremely steep in many places. We were warned to travel clockwise, and rumours reached our ears of cars that had skidded off the unguarded edge of some cliff into a valley hundreds of feet below. Travel was slow and inns were few, and on more than one occasion we had to ask the farmers and fishermen to put us up for the night, or to provide us with a meal.

Two years later, when we took the Gaspé tour for the second time, things were changing. Last summer the metamorphosis was complete.

The road has been widened throughout its 526 miles and all but 177 miles have been paved. Guard rails have been placed wherever necessary, steep grades have been reduced, bad curves have been improved. The thrill comes now from the magnificence of the scenery, not from the risks of the road.

A great many inns, cottages and cabins have been opened all along the way to accommodate the annual influx of sightseers. So whatever you may have heard of the difficulties involved in driving around the Gaspé we assure you that the hazards all belong to the past. Today you may go in either direction, and you will have no difficulty in finding delightful places to break the journey.

Not because of the roads, but because of the sun, we prefer to travel clockwise even today. The most beautiful views are along the St. Lawrence, and through the Shickshock Mountains, and no scenery looks its best if you have the afternoon sun in your eyes.

As you have no doubt found out, we do not often indulge in superlatives, but now we must, or we would be guilty of gross understatement. This is **the most spectacular drive in Quebec**. It is a truly memorable experience. We do not see how you could possibly be disappointed in it, if only you can be persuaded to give yourself time enough to enjoy it.

We once met some motor tourists in Florida who had come from California along the old Spanish Trail. We remarked that it was an interesting road. The husband who had done all the driving, looked blank.

(*Above*) The Gaspé Highway at Grande Vallée
(*Below*) Outdoor Bake-Oven Along the Gaspé Road

"Is it?" he said. "I wouldn't know. We covered over five hundred miles a day ever since we left home."

For the next two days all he wanted to do was sleep.

If you try to drive around the Gaspé in record time, you will not know, either, what it is all about. It can be done in two days, but we shudder at the thought. The taxis from Mont-Joli take four days, making three overnight stops en route. We seldom attempt the trip if we have not a week or ten days to spare. Last year we spent six nights on the way, and we felt as if we were hurrying.

Ste-Flavie - Mont-Joli (Population 5,000). The Gaspé tour officially starts at Ste-Flavie, a village on the St. Lawrence, or at the adjacent town of Mont-Joli, from which guided motor tours leave daily during the summer season.

Metis Beach, a few miles away, is usually our starting point, and sometimes we are tempted to stay in this attractive summer resort for so long that we get no farther. Metis was at one time a Scottish settlement, but the Scots soon left, or became absorbed, and today if you meet a Fraser or a Campbell you will probably have to address him in French.

Metis, however, is predominantly **a fashionable summer resort**. Many English-speaking Montrealers have beautiful cottages and gardens. They come back regularly each summer, and some families have been doing so for more than fifty years.

The Seaside House, one of our favourite hotels, reflects this trend. Most of the guests come back, year after year, to this comfortable and hospitable old inn. It overlooks the St. Lawrence which, at this point, is forty miles wide.

Equally attractive and popular is the Cascade Hotel,
also on the St. Lawrence. There are several other
pleasant inns and lodges strung along the highway, which
forms the main street of the village.

Metis is **a first rate resort for golfers, and for tennis
players**. The Cascade Golf and Tennis Club has a good
18 hole course, over 6,100 yards long, and eight tennis
courts, which are well maintained. There is a second 18
hole golf course at the Boule Rock Golf Club. Both
clubs are within easy walking distance of most of the
hotels. The Metis Beach Gift Shop, opposite the Cascade Hotel, has imported glass and china, woolens and
souvenirs.

Although the water temperature is seldom up to
sixty, some people bathe in the sea every day and seem
to enjoy it. The Matane River, twenty-five miles away,
is open to the public for **salmon fishing**, and there are
trout in many of the nearby streams.

After you leave Metis, the road runs close to the sea,
through **Baie-des-Sables** and the weather-beaten seaside
village of **St-Ulric**, to the town and the river of Matane.

Matane (Population 6,000). Our interest here centered
in the salmon fishing, although Matane is a substantial
commercial town, with an active lumber milling industry.
A daily ferry for cars and passengers crosses to Baie-
Comeau on the north shore of the St. Lawrence.

A stretch of twenty-six miles on the Matane River
has been opened to the public for salmon fishing. You
may fish from the banks or wade in the stream, but you
must fish with artificial flies. Fly-casting is the only
method allowed in Quebec for salmon fishing.

We saw our first salmon near the mouth of the river,
where the lumber company's dam crosses the stream.

There must have been six, at least, and each one looked as if it would tip the scales at more than twenty pounds. A fellow fisherman on the dam told us that he had caught seven salmon in that exact spot, earlier in the season.

"They are here," he said. "Look!" We had been looking for some time, thrilled by the sight of so many salmon together. "But they are not biting today," he added with finality, and he was right. Presently we moved above the dam, and we found that a secondary road follows the river upstream to the end of the fishing reserve.

Matane is one of the few places where the passers-by may **fish for salmon with a one day licence**. A number of very large fish have been caught recently in this river. It is well worth a try.

When you leave Matane behind you, there will be no more towns of any size until you have completed the circle around the Gaspé Peninsula, but every few miles— almost as if it were placed with mathematical precision— you will pass through a fishing village nestling in a sandy bay at the foot of a mountain. Each place has something unique about it, and yet they are alike in many ways. Each is at the mouth of some river or stream, each lies in the shadow of the Shickshock Mountains, and commercial fishing, in almost every case, is the major occupation of the inhabitants.

Ste-Félicité, Grosses-Roches, and Méchins are three such villages, and we do not have to tell you that they are all lovely enough to capture with your camera, or on canvas.

The Gaspé road has been photographed and painted by so many people that it is a familiar picture. But reproductions are not reality. They can not give you the sound of the surf breaking on the rocks, or the smell of the mountains and the sea, or the taste of a warm loaf of bread just baked in an outdoor oven.

We climbed to precipitous heights and dropped again to sea level. At **Capucins** the rocks have been beaten by the elements into strange shapes, resembling, as the name implies, the silhouette of a Capuchin monk.

Cap-Chat (Population 1,500). On the Rivière Cap-Chat there is a lumber mill, and along the highway you will find several shops, inns and cabins. Cap-Chat was one of the few villages that had hotel accommodation for tourists when the highway first went through, and it is still a popular stop.

The name of this town is always good for an argument. Some say it obviously refers to the rock formation of the headland, which they claim, looks like a cat. It is, we think, more likely to be a corruption of the name Chatte or Chastes, given to the cape by Champlain in honour of one of his friends.

Ste-Anne-des-Monts (Population 3,000) is an educational centre and one of the larger towns. We are always glad to find ourselves here at meal time. The Hotel Beaurivage on the main highway has a surprisingly **nice dining room**. They cook salmon, and other typical Gaspé food, just the way we like it. We think you will find it a pleasant stop for lunch or dinner.

The new Gaspesian Park is twelve miles south of Ste-Anne-des-Monts.

Le Parc de la Gaspésie is reached by a secondary road that follows the Ste-Anne River Valley up to Mt. Albert, one of the highest peaks in the Shickshock Mountains, the northern end of the Appalachian chain. The park covers an area of 1,300 square miles and comprises some of the highest mountains in Eastern Canada. Jacques-Cartier peak is 4,350 feet above sea level.

If you like **mountain climbing**, this is the place to come. The Department of Game and Fisheries has built **a hostelry** at the foot of Mt. Albert. Two trails lead to the top, where you may camp over night, at an altitude of 3,700 feet.

Other excursions are to Mt. Jacques-Cartier, five miles away, and to Lac des Américains where there is another **over-night shelter**. Here is a new thrill for the jaded traveller, something that few have done before you, something you will always remember.

The Mont-Albert Inn will supply an alpine guide for inexperienced mountain climbers. If you want to study the flora and fauna of the Shickshocks, this is the place to do it. It is necessary to make reservations in advance if you are planning to stay in the Gaspesian Park.

Because variety is still the spice of life, the sea looks particularly attractive after a sojourn in the mountains. At **St-Joachim-de-Tourelle, Ruisseau-Castor and Rivière-à-la-Martre** you will be back again to the rocky coast, to cod fish drying in the wind, to covered bridges and to a lumbering road that winds along the foot of the mountains, very close to the sea. After crossing the Rivière-à-la-Martre the road goes inland and climbs a hill from the top of which there is **an interesting panorama of the village and the lighthouse below**.

Beyond Marsoui the rock formations are fascinating. It is as if the bed of the ocean had rolled over, tilting the rocky cliffs until they are lying on their sides with the strata standing upright, or falling into fantastic curves.

Rivière-à-Claude comes down from Lac à Claude in the Parc de la Gaspésie, and at its mouth you will find another fishing village which, until a few years ago, could be reached only from the sea. It is called by the name of the river.

Mont-St-Pierre has a particularly pleasing setting in a bay, surrounded by mountains that rise from the water's edge. Last summer the settlement was busy building new cottages and inns for the Gaspé traveller, and we thought it would not be a bad place to stay if night were near.

It would be a great pity to go beyond this point in the dusk, and very foolish to attempt it in the dark, as some of the most beautiful scenery is yet to come, and some of the steepest and most winding roads are ahead of you.

If it is still light, you might like to drive on for another twenty-five miles to Madeleine-sur-mer, one of the best known over-night stops along this route, and one we think you will like. On the way you will pass through **Mont-Louis**, a fishing village which seems to be swinging away from cod in favour of lumbering and tourists.

We have noticed this happening in a number of places along the Gaspé road, during the past twenty years. Fishing and "making fish" still predominate, but the price of cod no longer controls the entire economy of the peninsula. The highway brings these villages into contact with the world beyond the mountains, and the coming of visitors has brought a modicum of prosperity in its wake.

We do not mean that the picturesque fishing village is a thing of the past. Far from it. You will still see cod fish drying on primitive flakes. Fishing boats are moored in every bay. Along the shore stand the simple and unadorned cottages of the fishermen, while on the cape, guarding and blessing the scene, is the church.

Even where a modern deep-freeze plant has been installed, or a row of new cottages has been built for the summer visitors, the spirit of the fishing villages has remained unchanged.

Gaspé has been described as a "land of history and romance", but you will look in vain for ancient houses of the French regime. Most of the parishes between Ste-Flavie and the Baie de Gaspé were founded in the nineteenth century. The architecture is uninspired—almost primitive. A house has four walls and a roof above, with little or no attempt to embellish it, but the composition of the whole—the mountains, the village and the sea—is magnificent.

Gaspé Peninsula has its ghost stories, and one of them relates to **Anse-Pleureuse**, the next village. "The Weeping Cove" was haunted for years by a ghost that terrified the fishermen with its wailing and groaning. A passing missionary discovered the cause—two trees, swaying against each other in the wind. He successfully stopped the weeping forever by chopping down one of the trees, but the ghost is commemorated in the name of Anse-Pleureuse.

We were impressed by the unusual rock formations in the cliffs between here and the fishing village of **Gros-Morne** and then, as we climbed another high hill, we found ourselves driving through pioneer farming country. A number of little boys called to us from the roadside: "Bateaux—twenty-five cents." They were all selling hand carved toy boats, some of which were beautifully made.

After passing through **Manche-d'Epée**—a new village where an old French sword handle was found by the settlers — you will come to the Madeleines — **Petite-Madeleine**, **Madeleine-Centre**, **Rivière-Madeleine**, and **Madeleine-sur-mer**. They are small places to have so many names. Some of the "Guided Gaspé Tours" stop here, and so do we, if it is meal time, or the end of the day.

Madeleine. Petite-Madeleine and Madeleine-Centre are on the heights. Be sure to notice the lighthouse as you pass, because you will probably want to walk out to visit the lighthouse keeper after supper. He welcomes visitors, will show you how the light works, and will tell you all about the fishing.

When you cross the bridge over the river, you will be in Rivière-Madeleine, sometimes referred to as Madeleine-sur-mer. This beautiful river comes down from the mountains in the Gaspesian Park. The Hotel du Golfe, with **overnight cabins** on the beach, was formerly a fish and game club, but now it is open to the public.

The Hotel Bon-Accueil is one of the old-timers, and through the years it has built up a big reputation for its cooking. You can enjoy such delicacies as cod's tongues and other famous Gaspé dishes, in a plain old-fashioned setting. Very satisfactory, and, as its name implies, you will be given a good welcome.

Across the road, directly on the beach, is Hotel Madeleine-sur-mer, with a row of new white cottages, modern in every way.

There are quite a number of **inns and cabins** in this area, and there is, of course, a small fishing settlement in the bay. This is fishing country, with trout in the rivers and cod in the sea, and guides and boats available in the village.

It is after leaving Madeleine that the real mountain

climbing begins for your car. The summit is reached about eight miles beyond the village, and then comes the long descent to **Grande-Vallée**, two miles below. There is a deep freezing plant here for fish, a harbour for small boats at the river mouth, and a church placed commandingly on a high cliff across the bay. Grande-Vallée has a small inn where you can stay, if you want to go out with the fishermen.

During the next twenty miles the highway passes through six villages, each busy making fish, which means placing salt cod on drying racks, or "flakes" and leaving them to cure in the wind. If you stop for a moment, you will be surrounded by friendly children, waiting to have their pictures taken, all asking innumerable questions, and not knowing a word of English among them.

You can see the island of Anticosti, if the day is clear, from **Pointe-à-la-Frégate**, **Cloridorme**, and the other fishing villages facing the Gulf of St. Lawrence. At **Grand-Etang** the road turns inland, beside the "big pond", and the scenery changes. The country is wild and unsettled, as the road winds through a mountain pass, leaving the line of the telephone and electric light poles.

L'Echourie is the next settlement of any size, and here, as at many of the fishing villages in this part of the country, the ancient ceremony of the blessing of the ships takes place in early summer. It is a vivid and impressive ceremony, all the fishing boats decorated with pennants, flowers, and streamers, and all the villagers dressed in their Sunday best. If you have only seen the boats and the villagers in their working attire, you will be amazed to see how fine they can look on an occasion like this.

Rivière-aux-Renards (Population 1,500). About a hundred years ago some Irish immigrants were wrecked near here, off the Cap-des-Rosiers. When they made shore they remained as settlers. Today many of the inhabitants of Fox River have Irish names, although they speak only French. The parish is one of the principal shipping ports for fish on the north Gaspé coast.

Many years ago, when the highway first opened, Fox River was one of the few villages with an inn. Since then it has become a town of some importance in this section of the country. The Château Gaspésien, opposite the church, is the town's **commercial hotel**. It serves a substantial mid-day dinner of country style food which we found quite satisfying. The hotel has a launch to take its guests out deep sea fishing.

The Caribou Inn, with **cabins on the beach**, is close to the fishing activities. We found it interesting to watch the **dogs hauling their small wagons** and working with their owners. The Gaspé dog is an important member of the family, and he seems to enjoy and to take pride in his elevated position.

The road divides at Rivière-aux-Renards. Highway 6A takes a short cut inland, via **St-Majorique**, a farming parish. By this route Gaspé is only seventeen miles away. The other road, Highway 6, continues along the coast to Cap-des-Rosiers and the new Cap-Bon-Ami Provincial Park. By this scenic shore road, the distance is thirty-nine miles between Rivière-aux-Renards and the town of Gaspé.

The Forillon and Cap-Bon-Ami Provincial Park. The point of land with the Gulf of St. Lawrence on one side and the Baie de Gaspé on the other is called the Forillon. The place names are descriptive: **Anse-à-la-Fougère**, Cove of the Ferns; **Anse-au-Griffon**, Cove of the *Griffon*, a ship that was wrecked off the treacherous point; **Anse-**

Jersey, settled by men from the Channel Islands. Champlain named the cape for the wild rose-bushes, a gentle name that belies the dangers of this rocky shore, where many ships were wrecked before the Cap-des-Rosiers lighthouse was built.

At **Cap-Bon-Ami** the provincial government has laid out a park, with some inspiring marine views. You will find **a tea room** there, for light refreshments.

The drive along the Baie de Gaspé makes everyone think of the first voyage of Jacques Cartier who, in July 1534, took shelter in this bay from a violent storm that lasted for several days. While stormbound, Cartier and his men built and erected an enormous wooden cross, thirty feet high, decorated with a shield bearing three *fleurs de lis* and inscribed with the words: "Vive le Roy de France". Indians gathered around him and watched with wonderment, and distrust, while Cartier claimed the land for the King of France; and Gaspé became known, for four hundred years, as the "Birthplace of Canada".

Now that it has become a province of the Dominion, Newfoundland will undoubtedly lay claim to the title of "Birthplace of Canada", for Cartier landed at Catalina Bay about two months before he planted his cross at Gaspé.

His real discovery of the place called Canada by the Indians—which lay between the Kingdom of the Saguenay and Hochelaga—was not made until the following year.

Gaspé (Population 2,000). The name seems to be derived from a Micmac Indian word meaning "the end", which referred, no doubt, to the tip of the peninsula.

On the outskirts of Gaspé, as you approach the town on Highway 6, there is **a small resort hotel**, built on a wooded promontory, high above the wharf and bathing beach. It is called the Battery Park Hotel, and we liked its log cabins in the woods, and its Gift Shop, which sells Quebec handicraft. Meals are served in the hotel dining room.

Baker's, the town's leading **commercial hotel**, has been popular since 1876. It has been well kept up, and it is a good place to stay if you are planning a fishing trip at this end of the Gaspesian Park. First Lake, recently opened to the public, is only five miles away, on the St. John River road, and it may be fished with a one day licence.

For a real trout fishing holiday, you will want to go right into the park, to Lake Adams, sixty miles from Gaspé, where there is a small camp, or to Lake Madeleine, still farther away, where there are **two fishing camps** run by the government on the American plan. There is an office of the Department of Game and Fisheries in the town of Gaspé where you can make reservations and get further information.

Next to Baker's Hotel, in a park-like square, you will see **a handsome stone cross**. It stands on the traditional site where Jacques Cartier erected his wooden cross, and it commemorates the four hundredth anniversary of that historic event.

One of the interesting sights we saw during our visit to the town of Gaspé was the **Provincial Government Fish Hatchery**. Some of the salmon in the pool for parents weigh over forty pounds. There are a great many smaller ponds where the young fish are kept until they are old enough to be placed in the lakes and rivers.

Gaspé is one of the few towns on the peninsula that was settled by United Empire Loyalists and in which a good percentage of English-speaking people still live.

During the two world wars Gaspé Basin was used as a military, naval and air base.

Boats leave from the town wharf for **Anticosti** Island, which is part of the Province of Quebec. It was on this island that the explorer, Louis Jolliet, built a fishing station towards the end of the seventeenth century. He asked help for this enterprise from King Louis XIV, claiming that it would give employment to many young men. There is good sport to be had **salmon fishing** on Anticosti. To arrange it, apply to the Consolidated Paper Corporation, Sun Life Building, Montreal.

It is not necessary to go as far as Anticosti to find good fishing. There are **salmon pools**, accessible by car, along the Port-Daniel and Little Cascapédia Rivers of Gaspé's southern shore. We shall tell you more about them when we take you on the drive along the Baie des Chaleurs.

Another pleasing place to stay is the Fort Prével Hotel, a little more than half an hour's drive from Gaspé. Once a military camp, Fort Prével is now a Provincial Park. **The hotel has restful cottage-like accommodations**, with a main lounge and dining room, tennis courts, and an expansive vista across the wide open sea, the only land visible being the tip of Cap Gaspé. If you like the sight and sound of the ocean, you will like Fort Prével.

At nearby **St. Peter's Point**, an old fishing port, a lighthouse on a rocky island guards the entrance to a miniature bay.

On rounding the point you get **your first glimpse of Percé Rock**, the highlight of every Gaspé tour. Artists come from the corners of the earth to paint the amazing scenery. Botanists climb Mont-Ste-Anne to study the rare plants found there. The geologically-minded speculate on the unusual rock formations, and the ornithologists

In the Town of Gaspé
The Jacques Cartier Cross.

find their Mecca on the bird sanctuary of Bonaventure Island.

A few people come to Percé, as Jacques Cartier did in 1534, to remain a day and go their way, apparently unimpressed. Beauty exists for us only if we take the time to see it. If you have come this far, we beg of you, do not hurry your departure. This is a place of rare and infinite beauty, but it is too vast to see at a glance, and too profound to understand in a moment. For most travellers, it is the answer to something they have long been seeking. What will it be for you?

[handwritten annotations:]

PERCÉ — P131 — P134 MoRaiies, climb MT ST anne
By endear road — "...Looked down on a sight that
cannot be excelled in all america" — P135.
PIC d'AuRoRe — walk to (SURPRISE 411) + Cap Bl
— Moon 1941 — P 136 demension of Perce Rock — see the
farming area — walk to it of low tide, it several
hundred feet from land — Fossils of Bozo —
Red conglomerate, Tordstone, limestone.
The old Indian Trail to St anne P 142 is a
Real — walk it or Jeep of stove By passing the
Cobble shores — 145 — Robin-Jones — whitman
could this feel took. 147 — "the captains House"
160 — On so to light house on Cap Blanc.

Chapter 16

PERCÉ ROCK AND BONAVENTURE ISLAND

THE APPROACH TO PERCÉ is one of the most spectacular things to be seen in this place of breath-taking beauty. The road goes through **Barachois**, the Gaspesian name for a sand bar. It is an Indian corruption of *barre* a bar, and *échouer,* to run aground.

From Barachois there is an unforgettable panorama— Bonaventure Island; The Rock; the jagged cliffs of La Muraille; the rose, grey and green of Mont-Ste-Anne.

After the first sight of The Rock, there are still many miles to drive into the village of Percé. You cross the long sand bar to the colourful settlement of **Coin-du-Banc**, at the corner of the reef. You climb up and into the mountains again, until you are directly above Percé, and there, suddenly spread out before you, is **the most spectacular view in all Gaspé**.

You will soon discover that Percé is more than a rock. The Rock is only one small part of the picture. And Percé is far, far more than a beautiful view. We think you will find enough of interest to be worth many hours of your time.

Percé (Population 1,500). The village has so much to offer, it is inconceivable that anyone, having come this far, would continue on his way without staying over for at least one night at Percé. You will probably want to stay much longer, if you are really interested in either rocks or birds.

There is **a wide range of accommodations** from

225

which to choose. We always find it difficult to decide which is the most interesting—to be directly on the beach, with a window looking out across the sea, or to be high in the hills, with the whole picture spread out before us.

The hotel and log bungalows of Au-Pic-de-l'Aurore, Peak o' Dawn, have a strong appeal. This is **a truly Gaspesian hotel**. Its design, its furniture, curtains, all things in it including the paintings on the walls, were created in Gaspé. The result is charming. The rooms in the hotel have private baths, and are pleasant, but we particularly liked the individual log cabins, with their stone fireplaces. They belong to the hotel, and you go to the main dining room for your meals. Pic-de-l'Aurore is the place to be if you have come to see the scenery, and the awe-inspiring spectacle of a sunrise over the ocean.

There are **two unusual beaches** at Percé, one on either side of the great rock. The first time we came to the village, both beaches were used almost exclusively for the landing and cleaning of fish. Now the south beach has been given over to tourists, and you will find a number of hotels and cottages along it.

We liked the Hotel La Normandie, which fronts on the ocean and backs on Chemin du Roi, the main street of the village. It, also, has carried out the Gaspesian idea in furnishings and decorations. The beach is at your door, for surf and sun bathing. La Normandie is run on the American plan. The dining room faces the sea, the Rock and Bonaventure Island. It is the largest of Percé's hotels, and the rooms on the ocean side are particularly nice.

A smaller beach hotel, also on the main street, is Hotel Percé. It has rooms in the main building and in

PERCÉ

(*Above*) You will soon discover that Percé is more than a rock.
(*Below*) North Beach and the jagged cliffs of La Muraille.

cottages, furnished in *habitant* style. Meals are served in the dining room at regular hours. Here, as at the Normandie, you may swim from the hotel.

There are many other places to stay, guest houses, cottages, small hotels, all clustered around the village and the Rock. You will surely be able to find accommodations that will please you.

The sights! Where would you like to begin? There are two celebrated mountains—Mont-Blanc with its great crevice, and Mont-Ste-Anne, nature's own botanical garden and an age-old place of pilgrimage. The trail to the top of Mont-Ste-Anne connects with the trail up Mont-Blanc, 1,300 feet high. Only one side of Mont-Ste-Anne can be climbed, as the other three sides are sheer rock. When you reach the top you will find several trails through the woods.

Each year, on the Festival of Sainte Anne, the people of Percé make a pilgrimage to the summit, continuing a custom which pre-dates the coming of the first missionaries. When the Récollets came to Percé, they found a cross already erected on Mont-Ste-Anne. It had undoubtedly been placed there by the Micmac Indians, although they knew nothing of Christianity. They made pilgrimages to Mont-Ste-Anne to watch the sun rise, for the sun was their god. Father Le Clercq, who came to Percé in 1675 to work among the Indians, found them wearing crosses as amulets, although they did not know why. Because of the crosses, he nick-named them the "Porte-Croix".

If you like to climb and to hike, you can seek rare plants on the mountains, and agates and fossils along the beaches. Looking for the agate stones, which came originally from the red conglomerates of Mont-Ste-Anne, makes a walk along the beaches something of an adventure.

Almost everyone who comes to Percé wants to paint or to photograph the picturesque capes. Cap Barré stands guard over the north beach. It joins with three jutting promontories, known as Trois Soeurs, and with Pic-de-l'Aurore to form "The Wall". When you see it, we are sure that you, too, will want to capture its unusual colours and contours on canvas or on film.

Other impressive capes are Mont-Joli, and Cap-Canon, probably named in honour of the Reverend Canon Albert de Prato, who was with John Rut's expedition to Newfoundland, in 1527, and who wrote a report of the voyage. He also gave his name to Percé Rock, which was originally called Cape Prato.

The Rock has changed greatly through the years. When Jacques Cartier passed this way, it was evidently still part of the mainland, as he referred to it as Cape Prato. About seventy years later, Champlain described it as "Isle Percé, a high rock with a hole through it." Father Le Clercq mentioned three arches, while Captain Smyth drew a picture of it, in 1760, clearly showing two. The arch seen by Champlain, which gave the rock its name, no longer exists. It collapsed about a hundred years ago, leaving an obelisk standing at the end of the Rocher Percé.

Millions of fossils are embedded within the strata of this great hulk, including some giant trilobites two feet in length.

There are stories told about people climbing the Rock, a hundred or more years ago, and using the top of it to grow hay. However that may be, today the walls are so steep that the top is inaccessible to man, and the Rock is inhabited only by birds.

When you have seen the mountains and the Rock, there is another adventure in store for you. The climax of every visit to Percé should be the boat trip to the world-famous bird sanctuary on Bonaventure Island.

Bonaventure Island. A hundred or more years ago, the island had a population of about two hundred. Its most colourful son was Captain Duval, the privateer, who sailed the seas under letters of marque from King George III of England and became the terror of all French merchantmen. When he retired from his adventurous career, Captain Duval settled on the Island of Bonaventure, where his descendants still live.

Today, including the Duvals, there are only about thirty people living on Bonaventure. It is occupied, however, by an estimated 60,000 birds. It lies three miles from the mainland and, except in stormy weather, it can easily be reached in small open boats. An ice bridge forms in the winter, connecting it with the village of Percé.

When the Gaspé Highway was first opened to the public, there were no excursion boats to take tourists out to see the Rock, Bonaventure and the Bird Sanctuary. It was necessary to make your own arrangements with one of the fishermen, and we think that is still the best way to go, if you wish to land on the island and to study and photograph the birds at your leisure.

If you are in a hurry, you may take one of the **regular excursion boats**, which run almost continuously all day and every day, except Sunday morning. They leave from both the North and South Beaches, circle the six mile circumference of Bonaventure Island passing close to the bird cliffs, and return to Percé. This trip, which

PERCÉ

(*Above*) Bonaventure Island from Pic-de-l'Aurore.
(*Below*) The South Beach.

is probably Gaspé's greatest tourist attraction, takes a little more than an hour.

Some years ago, when it became evident that the Gaspé Peninsula, and Percé in particular, was destined to become one of the major magnets for visitors to Quebec, the parish priest of Saint Michel de Percé warned his parishioners that the tourist industry, like everything human, carries within itself the germ of its own decay, and he urged them to ward off the dangers of standardization, to be faithful to their own ideals, and to remain unfailingly kind, courteous and hospitable.

The people of Gaspé have heeded his warning. Their hotels are truly Gaspesian, their hospitality renowned. In only one thing has there been any great standardization, and the crowds have made that almost inevitable. The boat trips, run as excursions to Bonaventure, have a flavour of commercialism about them. For the greatest enjoyment, make arrangements to go in a privately chartered boat, if you can, but if this is not possible, take one of the regular trips. It is something you must not miss.

The bird cliffs are on the ocean side of the island, not visible from the mainland. Federal and Provincial laws protect the birds and a commission is responsible for their care. Since 1919 it has been against the law to disturb the birds, or to interfere with them in any way. The precipitous red cliffs of Bonaventure, on which they nest, rise abruptly from the water and form a natural protection, almost like a fort, on the ocean side. The only way that human beings can approach the birds is by landing on the low side and walking across the island to the cliffs, which have been aptly called "the largest apartment house in the world".

The Bird Sanctuary. The birds begin to arrive from the south about the middle of April, while there is still snow on the ground, and some of them do not migrate until November. Birds of the gull family will remain as long as they can find food.

Gulls (*Family Laridae*). By far the most numerous are the Herring Gulls (*Larus argentatus*). There are about 25,000 of them nesting in colonies on Bonaventure, Percé Rock and Cap Barré. We have seen them so thick, following a fishing boat ashore, that they were like clouds in the sky. A full grown bird is white, with a grey mantle and black primaries, has a wing spread of 56 inches and is about two feet in length. The young birds are grey. They have a noisy cry—a shrill and harsh "Cack-cack-cack".

You may see a few Great Black-backed Gulls (*Larus marinus*), although they are not common on Bonaventure. They are the largest of the family, about two and a half feet long, with a wing spread of 66 inches.

The smallest gull is the Kittiwake (*Rissa tidactyla*), only 16 inches in length, with a wing spread of thirty-five inches. They can be distinguished by their size, and by their black feet. The gulls usually lay and hatch three eggs.

Gannets (*Family Sulidae*). Bonaventure has one of the world's largest Gannet colonies, with an estimated twenty thousand Gannets (*Sula bassana*) nesting here each year. These enormous white birds, with black primaries, bills and feet, measure thirty-five inches in length and have a wing spread of six feet. They nest on piles of sea-weed on the rocky ledges, each nest containing only one egg. A gannet reputedly eats its own weight in fish every day—approximately twelve pounds. In spite of their gluttonous habits, they live for fifty years or more. They leave in September to winter farther south at sea, seldom coming on land.

Cormorants (*Family Phalacrocoracidae*). There are approximately five thousand Double-crested Cormorants (*Phalacrocorax auritus*) on Bonaventure Island during the breeding season. They are large birds, two and a half feet in length, with a wing spread of 60 inches. Their long necks, heads and underparts are glossy black, the throat pouch is orange yellow, and they have long curved beaks. Their nests contain three or four bluish-green eggs.

Auks, Murres, and Puffins (*Family Alcidae*). There are about three thousand of these birds which resemble penguins, with their short legs, white breasts and blackish mantles, but each has marked characteristics of its own. The Razor-billed Auk (*Alca torda*) has a white line across its short, flat bill, while the Murre (*Uria troille*) has a long, pointed bill with no markings. Both birds have brownish throats in the summer, both are sixteen inches long with a wing spread of thirty inches.

The Puffin (*Fratercula arctica*) is often called the Sea Parrot, and we hope you will be lucky enough to see some of these amusing birds that look like clowns, with their very large red and yellow bills, and their bright red feet. We saw only two, but there are sometimes as many as a thousand on the island. They seldom, if ever, come to the mainland. Each year, the females of this family lay and hatch a single egg, on the bare and rocky cliffs. The cry of the Puffin is hoarse and low, like a weird croak or groan.

234

Guillemots and Petrels. Other birds which you may see, but which do not come in large numbers to Bonaventure, are the Leach Petrels (*Oceandroma leucorhoa*), 8 inches long with dark brownish grey plumage, and white tail coverts. The Black Guillemots (*Cepphus grylle*) called by the French "pigeons de mer", are black in summer, except for their red legs and white patches on their wings. Their cry is a piercing whistle or squeal. The Black Guillemot does not build a nest but lays two eggs in rocky crevices.

The birds return to the sanctuary generation after generation and unless some catastrophe disturbs them, they will continue to do so, and to increase in number.

This brief guide to the birds you will see is by no means exhaustive or complete, but if you are an inexperienced bird watcher we hope that it will help you to distinguish one family from another.

A few ardent ornithologists have been known to spend their nights, as well as their days, on Bonaventure Island, to be as near as possible to the birds, but most of you will be willing and content to return to your comfortable hotel at Percé.

Back in the village, if you have some shopping to do for gifts, we think you will like the Black Whale, **a charming little shop** which sells native handicrafts and uses the profits for worth-while community projects. The Arts Domestiques and the Linwol Shoppe also sell handicrafts. There are a number of other stores where you can buy Kodak films, post cards and souvenirs.

If you have watched the sunrise from the rosy Pic-de-l'Aurore—if you have stood on top of Mont-Ste-Anne, looking west across the Shickshocks and east to the far horizons of the sea—if you have strolled at high noon along the warm sand of the beaches looking for fossils and agate stones, and swum in the cool invigorating ocean—if you have walked out, at low tide, to get a close-up view of the Rock, and have gone in a boat to see and hear the birds of Bonaventure—if you have done all these things, you can truly say: "I have seen Percé", and tomorrow we can continue our tour of Quebec.

Chapter 17

SALMON FISHING ALONG THE
BAIE DES CHALEURS

THE BAIES DES CHALEURS would be a good place for Americans to celebrate the Fourth of July. It was on that date, in 1534, that Jacques Cartier sailed into the bay, looking for a passage to China. Because it was the height of the hot summer season, he named it the Baie des Chaleurs.

It is **a pleasant and peaceful country**, lacking some of the grandeur of the mountain scenery along the northern shore of the peninsula, but making up for it with a fine climate, usually free of fog, and with beaches where the water is warm enough for everyone to enjoy the bathing.

The highway is paved all along this coast. It runs through rural parishes, with every few miles a miniature man-made harbour to shelter the fishing boats from the storms. **Anse-à-Beaufils** has one of these havens, and there is another at **Ste-Thérèse-de-Gaspé**, both colourful enough to tempt any artist to linger.

Grande-Rivière has a larger harbour, also man-made, two biology stations, and a school of fishery. **Pabos** is another fishing village, its name being Micmac for "quiet water".

Chandler (Population 2,000). This industrial town at the mouth of the Grand Pabos River concerns itself chiefly with pulp wood, but it is also the shopping centre for the adjacent farming area.

C. Langlois has a camp and territory under lease for **speckled trout fishing**.

A covered bridge crosses the south-west branch of the Pabos, a pretty, pebble-bottomed river emptying into a deep bay, across which there is a good vista of the town.

Presently the road climbs up above the sea, and you can look down on a lighthouse guarding the minute harbour, and watch the waves breaking on the rocky shore. There is a wooded island off **Newport**, where sea birds often gather. A few miles beyond you will come to **Anse-au-Gascon**, which marks the spot where the ocean ends and the Baie des Chaleurs begins.

Salmon Fishing. The fame of the Baie des Chaleurs has spread far and wide as one of the best places in North America to angle for the greatest sporting fish of them all—the Atlantic Salmon.

Formerly the fishing rights on the rivers flowing into the bay were privately leased, and there was little chance for anyone to fish these waters if he did not belong to a club. Recently, however, the Quebec government has opened two of these celebrated rivers to the public. The Department of Game and Fisheries has established **fishing camps at strategic points, and guides are available.** The season begins on the first of May and continues until the fifteenth of October.

A non-resident fishing licence for Atlantic Salmon and all other fish costs $15.50 for the season. It is valid for husband and wife, and for all children under eighteen years of age. A three day licence is $5.25. For all fish except Atlantic Salmon the season licence costs $5.25.

Port-Daniel, a village on the river of the same name, is the entrance to one of these salmon fishing reserves. The other is on the Petite-Cascapédia River, fifty-five miles farther up the bay.

At the crossroads in the centre of the village of Port-Daniel, you will see a sign which reads:

Department-Chasse-Pêche
Réserve de pêche
Salmon and Trout Fishing
Camp   5 miles

The road indicated by the sign runs up the Port-Daniel River for six miles, and you will find that there are **several salmon pools** which can be fished from the bank. At the end of the road there are **two fishing camps** belonging to the Department of Game and Fisheries, and trails which lead to other salmon pools. The camp **dining room** serves meals to anyone who is fishing the river.

If you prefer, you may stay in the village, or anywhere else along the coast within motoring distance, and drive in to fish these waters during the day. Port-Daniel and Matane are the only two salmon rivers we know of which can be reached by car and fished with a one day licence.

The Manoir St-Georges, open all year, is a commercial hotel in the centre of the village. There are other small hotels, and several over-night cabins, which offer country fare, pleasant rural scenery, and easy access to the salmon fishing.

One of our favourite holiday spots is nineteen miles away, in the interesting fishing village of Paspébiac.

Paspébiac is a Micmac name, meaning "a broken shoal". The Park Inn, set in spacious woods with an attractive garden, is **a unique guest house** which we are sure you will like. It has such good meals and is so well run that it has already gained renown, although it has only been going for a year or two.

The house was formerly the home of the manager of Robin, Jones and Whitman Company, Limited. This firm was established at Paspébiac in 1766 by Charles Robin from Jersey. It is one of the real pioneers in chain store merchandising and the second oldest company in Canada, being topped only by "The Governor and Company of Adventurers of England Trading into Hudson's Bay".

The old house where Charles Robin lived still stands. Somewhat altered and enlarged, it now serves as the office for the Quebec headquarters of the company. You will find it down by the fishing wharves, the centre of activity for one of the largest cod fishing and processing plants in Canada.

The great mass of nets you will see spread out along the wharves to dry are used only for catching bait. The fishing is done with hand lines.

This is a fine place to see the cod fishing industry in action, and at close range. We watched the men packing salt cod in 100 lb. boxes to be shipped to Italy. In another building the fish were being filleted and packed in cartons for quick freezing. Here, as at many of the fishing ports of Gaspé, the government operates a deep freeze plant where the fishermen can keep their bait as well as store their frozen fillets.

Paspébiac, being between the Port-Daniel and the Cascapédia Rivers, is a convenient as well as a delightful place to stay if you have come to Quebec for the salmon fishing.

There is also speckled **trout fishing** to be had in the nearby rivers, and duck and partridge (ruffed grouse) **shooting in season**.

If you are staying at the Park Inn, Major Overing, the proprietor, will tell you where to go for the best hunting and fishing, and where you can get experienced guides.

New Carlisle (Population 1,400). The fine old Court House on the main street, which looks like a wooden building but actually is solid stone boarded over, proclaims this to be the county town for Bonaventure. The town was founded by United Empire Loyalists, and many of the original settlers now rest in peace in the graveyard of the Anglican Church. With them lies "Colonel Isaac Mann, who departed this life on the 25th of December, 1803".

Like so many U. E. Loyalists, he had fought for the King in the Revolutionary War, was banished from his home, and had come to Canada with his family to start a new life, everything he owned and held dear left behind him forever.

New Carlisle was originally an English-speaking community, but, like Gaspé, French has now begun to predominate.

St-Bonaventure has fishing in its river, warm sea bathing on a shallow beach—particularly suitable for children—and limited accommodations in small inns and cabins.

St-Charles-de-Caplan is a farming community, where some of the women still do their spinning on old-fashioned spinning wheels. We enjoyed watching them. There are several new and modern cabins at Caplan, in nice locations along the beach.

About ten miles beyond you will come to one of the real highlights of Gaspé, the fishing rivers of Petite and Grande-Cascapédia.

New Richmond is on the Petite-Cascapédia River, as fine a place to fish for salmon as you are likely to find. These waters, formerly leased to private clubs, are now open to the public. Through the Department of Game and Fisheries at Quebec, you can arrange for camp accommodation, guides and canoes to fish this celebrated stream.

The trip up and down the Petite-Cascapédia River requires five days. You drive to the first camp, about five miles north of New Richmond and leave your car there. You ascend the river to the forks, about fifteen

(Top) GRANDE-CASCAPÉDIA RIVER
(Middle) ROBIN, JONES & WHITMAN FISHERY AT PASPÉBIAC
(Bottom) THE PARK INN, PASPÉBIAC

miles farther upstream, in twenty-four-foot salmon-fishing canoes, poled along by two guides. **Rustic camps** have been built near the fishing pools. As you descend the river, you will pass again through the salmon pools.

The salmon do not go beyond the forks, but there is good fishing to be had for trout in most of the branches of these rivers. You can get **a fishing permit** from the government agent at New Richmond to go up the Casca-pédia Road to Berry Mountain Lake to fish for speckled trout. It is necessary to take food supplies with you on this trip, and a guide is desirable. These can be obtained through Campbell's store, at Cascapédia. The special licence is $2.00 a rod, and the guide is $7.00 a day.

As long as you have a licence, there are no restrictions against fishing the tidal waters of the river, from Grande-Cascapédia to the sea.

You will find a fair amount of **over-night accommodation** in the village of New Richmond, in small hotels and in cabins, including the Chalet Francis' fifteen log bungalows on the Petite-Cascapédia River.

Shortly after you leave New Richmond you will cross the Grande-Cascapédia River on a long and unusually picturesque red **covered bridge**. Here you enter the Micmac Indian Reserve, and whenever you stop Indian children will swarm around you, offering baskets and whisks for sale. The next village is **Maria**, a charming little place with a good beach, good fishing, and a light-house on the long wharf.

Carleton-Sur-Mer is a popular summer resort. It was founded in 1756 by Acadians, and was called Tracadi-gèche—"the place where the herons abound". The English re-named it in honour of Guy Carleton, Lord

Dorchester, Governor-General of Canada, but it has remained predominantly French.

There is **a handicraft shop** on the main street, which sells Tremblay hooked rugs, St-Jean-Port-Joli wood carvings, and hand-woven articles from all over Quebec.

Carleton-sur-mer makes a satisfactory over-night stop. There are several hotels, a beach, and a 9 hole golf course. The Hotel des Sables Rouges, facing the sea, has comfortable rooms in the main building, at reasonable rates, and some pretty red and white cottages for those who want more privacy.

Behind the hotel there is farm land, with cows and horses grazing, and beyond that a wooded mountain. If you climb the mountain, you will find a Shrine to Saint Joseph at its summit.

One of the oldest salmon fishing associations in Canada is at Carleton-sur-mer, La Société Co-op des Pêcheurs de Carleton. They specialize in packing Gaspé salmon in sea-weed and ice and shipping them all over the country. If you want to send an eight or ten pound salmon to your friends at home, this company will pack and ship it for you.

After you leave Carleton, you will notice more farms, more logging, and fewer fishing villages. At **St-Jean-l'Evangéliste**, on the Rivière-Nouvelle, you can, if you wish, turn off the highway and follow a gravel road to Pointe Miguaska, where **a ferry** runs across the bay to Dalhousie, in New Brunswick.

Pointe Miguaska is really the end of the Baie des Chaleurs. From here to Ste-Anne-de-Restigouche it is called Restigouche Bay, and beyond that it is the river. At this end of the Baie des Chaleurs, near **Pointe-à-la-**

Garde, the last naval battle of the Seven Year's War in North America was fought in 1760.

Pointe-à-la-Croix is the turn-off for the old mission settlement of **Ste-Anne-de-Restigouche**, founded by the Récollets to convert the Micmac Indians, about three hundred years ago. Today it is an Indian Reserve, with a fine church, a monastery, and a restoration of the old Récollet well.

We have come to the end of the Baie des Chaleurs, but by no means have we come to the end of the salmon fishing. At the head of the Restigouche Bay, two of the world's most famous salmon rivers find their way to the sea—the Restigouche River and its tributaries, leased to the Restigouche Club, and the Matapédia River, where in the right season, with the right guide, and with any kind of luck, you will have some of the best salmon fishing of your life.

Chapter 18

THE MATAPÉDIA VALLEY

A HUNDRED YEARS AGO the Matapédia Valley was a wilderness of forests, inhabited by moose, deer and caribou, and of streams that were the spawning ground for Atlantic salmon. The coming of the railroad and the highway brought settlers and tourists, but in many places the original character of the valley has remained.

Some of the finest salmon fishing in Canada is to be had in the Restigouche and the Matapédia Rivers, which meet in the village of Matapédia.

Matapédia is known far and wide as the headquarters of the famous Restigouche Salmon Fishing Club, whose membership is made up largely of prominent Americans, and whose club house you will see on Highway 6 as you enter the village. This club has leased the fishing rights on the Restigouche River and its tributaries, and its members fish these waters until the middle of August, when the season closes.

The village is at the cross-roads of travel. It is a railway junction point, and **the only bridge across the Restigouche River is here.**

Although you may not fish in the Restigouche, there are a number of pools along the Matapédia River, privately leased, that can be fished by making arrangements with the owners.

The Hotel Restigouche has **salmon fishing** waters under lease, about thirty miles up the river. They also have a camp for moose and deer hunting in season. They will arrange your hunting and fishing holiday for you, and supply you with guides and equipment. We found it most convenient, and about the easiest way possible to have a day or two of salmon fishing on this celebrated river.

As well as catering to the hunter and the fisherman, the Restigouche Hotel is popular with motorists. On our first visit to Matapédia we were amazed to find such a large, modern fireproof hotel in such a small village. It is a combination of commercial and resort hotel, and it will please you if you like city conveniences even when you are on your vacation.

About eight miles up the Matapédia Valley you will come to the Matapédia Hotel, which offers good salmon fishing on leased waters, formerly part of the domain of the late W. E. Corey, president of the U. S. Steel Corporation. These waters have recently been leased by Dr. J. Howard Macdonell, of Matapédia. If you wish to fish them, the rates are $25.00 a day per rod, plus $9.00 for boat and guide. The rates may seem high, but think what it would cost you to belong to one of the salmon fishing clubs!

The Matapédia Hotel is also open to non-fishermen at reasonable rates.

The paved highway runs northward following the river valley through the mountains, and passing several private fishing camps on its way to **Routhierville**, a small mountain resort with cabins and bungalows for overnight guests. The hotel is a bus stop.

Around **Ste-Florence**, the next settlement, some of the land has been cleared, and beyond this the hills gradually flatten out into rolling farming country.

Causapscal is a lumbering town, with hotels, shops, garages, a theatre and a big, showy church built in 1910. A sign on the main street warns the motorist: "Pas de Stationnement", which reminded us that we would soon be back to civilization where "No Parking" was the order of the day on all main streets. There is good hunting and fishing in the nearby hinterland. If you are interested you can get in touch with Pierre D'Anjou, at the Club de Chasse et de Pêche Causapscal, who has territory under lease fifteen miles from the town for fishing, and for moose, deer and bear hunting. The best time to fish here is in June and July.

H. A. Pelletier, of The Nouvel Hotel Bellevue, Causapscal Station, also has territory under lease at the "18 Mile Fishing Club", fourteen miles from Causapscal. He can offer you **speckled trout fishing and hunting in season**.

Lac-au-Saumon is a widening of the Matapédia River. In the village of the same name, across a covered bridge, there is a Shrine to Saint Joseph.

Amqui (Population 3,000) is the county town and the shopping centre for an agricultural parish. Just north of it lies Lac Matapédia, the source of the river. In this part of Quebec no one bothers to translate the signs into English. It is a pity, because quite a number of tourists might not realize that "Chalets à louer" means that there are cottages for rent on this charming lake with its pretty wooded islands.

Val-Brillant has a handsome stone church and a pleasing location on Lac Matapédia. **Sayabec**, at the northern end of the lake, is a farming and lumbering village.

Here you leave behind you the Matapédia Valley as you go over the divide. About half an hour farther along you will come to **Mont-Joli** and to the village of **Ste-Flavie**. There you will see, once again, the broad St. Lawrence spread out before you.

The return trip to Lévis is made over the same road we covered in Chapter 14, so there is no need to retrace it in detail. It is a little over two hundred miles from Ste-Flavie to the Quebec Bridge. **You can vary the route** by taking the high road between **Andréville** and **Ste-Anne-de-la-Pocatière**, through the pleasant rural villages of **St-Pascal** and **St-Pacôme**.

And so the circle has been completed. The Gaspé Tour has become a memory, and in the very nature of things our memories fade with time, whether they be gay or sad. We predict, however, that you will long remember the Gaspé Road, Percé Rock and the birds of Bonaventure. If you were lucky enough to land a Gaspé salmon, we are certain that it will take more than time to make you forget a thrill like that!

Part Six

HIGHLIGHTS IN THE EASTERN TOWNSHIPS

Chapter 19

TOURING "LES CANTONS DE L'EST"

ROAD LOG FOR HIGHWAYS 23 AND 1
From Quebec to Montreal, via
Sherbrooke and the Lake District

Miles

0   Quebec - Lévis. Follow Hy. 23

10 St-Henri - Turn right. Hy. 53 goes
to Lac Etchemin

36 Beauce - Valley Junction - Follow
Hy. 1. Route 23 goes to Maine

67 Thetford Mines - Asbestos

72 Black Lake

90 Garthby - Lake Aylmer

119 East Angus

133 Sherbrooke - Junction for Hys. 1, 5,
& 22. Go south on Hy. 5 for Lennoxville, North Hatley and Lake
Massawippi

149 Magog - Lake Memphremagog

170 Waterloo - Go south on Hy. 39 for
Knowlton and Brome Lake

182 Granby

232 Montreal

THE EASTERN TOWNSHIPS, or Les Cantons de l'Est, are a
continuation northward of the States of Vermont, New
Hampshire and Maine, from which they are separated

only by the higgledy-piggledy international boundary line between the United States and Canada.

The name "Eastern Townships" is rather confusing, as these townships are by no means in the eastern end of Quebec. The name first appears in print in the *Quebec Almanac* for 1806.

The first man to write about the Eastern Townships was the Reverend Charles Stewart, Minister of St-Armand, who in 1815 described them as "extending east from the River Richelieu." The exact area contained in the Townships, however, has always been rather vague.

The name *Cantons de l'Est* applies only to the townships which were opened for settlement after 1791, the year that the country was divided into Upper and Lower Canada. There are, therefore, no towns or villages in the Eastern Townships which belong to the French regime, nor are there any United Empire Loyalist settlements.

Loyalists were specifically forbidden in 1783 to build homes in this area, for fear of friction with the Vermonters. In spite of the law, a few settlers came, but Sir Frederick Haldimand, the governor, ordered them to be removed, and threatened to destroy any other Loyalist houses that were built here.

So the Eastern Townships remained uninhabited until the law was changed, in 1791, when American, Scottish, English and French settlers began to pour in. Today it is one of the most densely populated sections of the province, and an intricate network of highways and roads covers the entire area.

We have chosen the paved routes as those you will most likely want to follow, but there are some interesting by-ways, especially around Lake Memphremagog, which you may want to explore.

Some of the highest mountains, the prettiest lakes

and the most delightful resorts lie in these **Cantons de l'Est**.

Lac Etchemin. The most easterly of the lake resorts, and one that is apt to be overlooked because it is not on a through highway, is Lac Etchemin, at the head of the Etchemin River Valley. It is about fifty miles south of Lévis, on a paved road. Le Manoir du Lac Etchemin, at Ste-Germaine, is quite a charming little place in a rural dairy farming setting in the mountains. Mont Orignal has an altitude of over 2,000 feet. Le Manoir is modern, has good French cooking, and is a particularly nice place for **fresh water swimming**. Rates by the week are reasonable.

Chaudière River Valley. In flood season the falls on this river can be spectacular. You crossed the mouth of the Chaudière near the Quebec Bridge. Route 1 follows it closely as far as Valley Junction. At **Ste-Maxime-de-Scott**, a real French Canadian habitant farming village, as pretty as it can be, there are **a few small inns** offering over-night accommodation of a rural type, mostly in cabins.

Ste-Marie (Population 2,500) is one of the largest towns in the Chaudière Valley, and it is still growing. It crowds along the narrow main street, following the river. Ste-Marie is the centre for a prosperous farming area. All around it there is pretty rural scenery of considerable charm—cattle grazing—neat and well-kept farmhouses with big barns of an unusual square design—pretty reflections in the calm water of the river. The town is a pleasant place to stop for a meal or for the night.

At **Beauce** or **Valley Junction** the routes separate. Highway 23 continues on to the border of Maine, while

Highway 1 crosses the Chaudière and heads for the lake district around Sherbrooke. The river has its source in Lake Megantic, eighty miles away. It was along this valley that Benedict Arnold and his men made their ill-fated march to Quebec, during the American Revolution.

About half an hour after we left the valley of the Chaudière, we found ourselves in the heart of the **asbestos country**. At **East Broughton** and at **Robertson-ville** there were mountains, some of them natural hills, but many of them great man-made mounds of slag from the asbestos mines.

Most of the world's supply of long-fibre asbestos comes from the Eastern Townships of Quebec, and the biggest and most important quarries of all are to be found in and near Thetford Mines.

Thetford Mines (Population 15,000) has wide streets, a modern residential section, several large shops and a fine stone city hall. Nevertheless, it has all the earmarks of being a "boom town", and it is much more concerned with mining than it is with catering to visitors.

Asbestos was discovered here over a hundred years ago, but it was not mined commercially until 1877. Today the greenish-grey dust from the mills seems to be over everything, and there are great yawning gaps in the ground that look like the craters of extinct volcanoes. Mine shafts, ugly and weather-beaten, stand guard over man-made mountains of slag.

Thetford Mines has **a golf course** and there are some lovely country places near the town, but beyond, at **Black Lake**, you come to more quarries, more towering slag piles, and the inevitable mutilation of the countryside that always goes with large scale mining activities.

At the town of **Disraeli** we came to Lake Aylmer,

which runs east of the highway for the next ten miles or so. We were surprised to find so few summer resorts along this pretty stretch of water. There is a small settlement at **Garthby**, and there are some housekeeping cabins for rent, with boats on Lake Aylmer, near **St-Gérard**.

Lake Aylmer was named in honour of Lord Aylmer who, in 1831, visited the Eastern Townships and wrote the British Secretary of State to say that he thought this section of Canada could support 500,000 persons. His letter resulted in the formation of the British-American Land Company which obtained large grants of land in the Eastern Townships and sent out settlers, mostly from the Highlands of Scotland.

The name **East Angus** commemorates the coming of the Scottish settlers. It is a pulp and paper town, and true to its Scottish tradition it has **a golf course**.

As we passed through **Ascot Corner**, a scenic spot on the St. Francis River, we wished we had brought along a picnic. The river has islands, and probably fish, as it flows out of three lakes, Aylmer, St. Francis and Lac-à-la-Truite. We crossed the river again as we entered Sherbrooke.

Sherbrooke (Population 50,000). On the outskirts of the city, as we approached it from the east, we came to the Royal Cabins, **a well-planned cottage colony** for over-night guests. In the centre of the lawn there is a swimming pool, which looks inviting on a hot day. The café in connection is of the quick-lunch-soda-fountain variety, and quite satisfactory.

Sherbrooke is a pleasant small city, which is rapidly growing into a big city. It is well ordered, showing considerable civic pride, and it has a lot to offer the visitor.

The 65th annual Fair was in progress when we were last there, at the end of August, and for anyone interested in live stock, agriculture, industry, or just in having fun, it is a first rate show. A typical Eastern Townships exhibit is **the maple products—sugar and syrup**—for which this part of Quebec is famous. The Exhibition Park is on East Sherbrooke Street, on a hill overlooking the valley of the St. Francis River. During the Fair, as well as at other seasons of the year, harness races are held on the half mile track.

The city is bi-lingual now, although the original settlers were English and American. It was named after Sir John Coape Sherbrooke, a general in the War of 1812, and Governor of Canada in 1816.

As you come down the hill on Highway 1, and cross the bridge over the St. Francis River, you will see an **Information Bureau** on your left, opposite the New Sherbrooke Hotel. The hotel is an old-timer, big and commercial, but it has been well kept up. We thought the meals were very good, and the various club rooms lively.

Just a block up the hill from the New Sherbrooke Hotel, at the corner of King and Wellington Streets, is the centre of the shopping district. It is also the junction of the main highways passing through the city. Route 1 continues up King Street, and on it there is as pretty a floral arrangement as we remember seeing in the business section of any city. **A mosaic of flowers** has been planted along the central boulevard. The absence of street cars and pole lines also adds to the attractiveness of Sherbrooke.

West on Highway 1, there is **a better than average drive-in restaurant** called Olivier's, where you can get almost anything, from a cup of coffee or an ice cream

SHERBROOKE
A mosaic of flowers along the central boulevard.

soda to a full course dinner. The dining room is attractively panelled in pine, and there is ample parking space all around the building.

Visitors to Sherbrooke are invited to play on the **18 hole golf course** and to use the dining room of the Sherbrooke Country Club, which can be reached by going up King Street West, and north on Prospect Street.

Although we like Sherbrooke and wish that more industrial cities were as pleasant, we usually head for one of the lakes if we expect to be in this neighbourhood for long. We are particularly attracted to the charming resort village of North Hatley, on Lake Massawippi, about twelve miles south of Lennoxville.

Lennoxville (Population 2,500), a residential and educational suburb of Sherbrooke, lies three miles to the south on Highway 5, the main travelled route between Vermont and Quebec. It is a leisurely town, with an academic Victorian air about it. You might enjoy staying in one of the cabin colonies, if you are ready for a rest.

North Hatley, on Lake Massawippi, about twelve miles beyond Lennoxville, is one of our favourite resorts—summer or winter. We think it is a particularly pretty village, and it can offer you whatever kind of accommodations you may want. In the summer-time you will find the **tennis courts** in play, the **golf course** of the Massawippi Country Club busy with tournaments, the lake alive with people **sailing and swimming**. There is no trick to acquiring a canoe, or even a sailboat, if you feel like competing in one of the regular racing events.

North Hatley is a friendly place, small enough to make you feel at home as soon as you arrive. It is **a lively, sporting village in the winter-time**, too, with **ski**

tows and down-hill runs on Green Timber Mountain. **Ice boating** is good on Lake Massawippi, and there is skating on flood-lighted rinks.

Brae Manor, on a hill overlooking the lake, is the kind of **guest house** we are always seeking, but rarely find. We were delighted with its club-like atmosphere, its cozy bar, and its comfortable rooms. Brae Manor has a **yacht club**, where you may swim or indulge in **water skiing or sailing**. In the winter you can use the ski tow right in front of the house, if you do not want to go as far as the Green Timber Mountain. This hospitable inn is open all year, and we do not know of a nicer place to spend a holiday, at reasonable rates.

Hovey Manor is **a new luxury inn** just south of the village, on the lake. It is the show place of North Hatley. Formerly a private country estate, reminiscent of George Washington's Mount Vernon, it was just getting into its stride as a guest house when we were there last summer. Many of the bedrooms have wood-burning fireplaces, all have private baths and are charmingly furnished. The public rooms and the gardens are beautiful. Hovey Manor should prove to be a happy addition to North Hatley's wide range of interesting hotels, inns and guest houses.

It is not a major feature of the place, but we should mention **the fishing**. We know the bass are big in Lake Massawippi because a five-and-a-half pounder was landed at our feet on the wharf of Hovey Manor.

In the winter-time, if you want to be right in the heart of the **ski runs** you might like to stay at the Auberge Hillcrest Lodge, on the slope of Green Timber Mountain, about three miles from the village. There are five ski tows, and numerous downhill and slalom runs, for experts and beginners. There is a pro to instruct you, and you will find a sporting ski-club atmosphere at the Hillcrest Lodge. The rates are moderate.

To round out the winter activities at North Hatley, the venturesome may go **ski-joring**, while the less energetic may follow in a horse-drawn sleigh.

North Hatley is not *Le Vieux Québec*. It has little of the old French regime about it. Its principal hotels are English speaking, and as the Vermont border is only twenty miles away, a number of Americans spend their holidays here. Although not entirely typical of the Province of Quebec, North Hatley is a delightful place. At least, we think so.

Some of the by-roads in the vicinity are worth exploring. At **Waterville**, about ten minutes away to the east, there is a 9 hole golf course, and at **Compton**, not far beyond, a fashionable girls' school. Westward there are the beauties of Lake Memphremagog, with fishing clubs at **Georgeville**, where good catches of **landlocked salmon and rainbow trout** are taken every summer.

Lake Memphremagog is thirty miles long and straddles the international boundary line between Quebec and Vermont. Its principal town, on the Quebec side, is Magog.

Magog (Population 10,000). The name has nothing to do with the Biblical Gog and Magog but is merely an abbreviation of what the Indians called the lake. Memphremagog means "the beautiful water".

Magog is an industrial town, at the northern end of the lake. It is an old summer resort, which has taken a new lease of life in winter with the opening of nearby **Mount Orford Park** for skiing and snow shoeing. The mountain rises to a peak of 2,860 feet, and it has one of

EASTERN TOWNSHIPS

(*Top*) Knowlton Golf Club, Brome Lake.   (*Middle*) Hovey Manor, North Hatley.
(*Bottom*) Brae Manor, North Hatley.

the longest and fastest downhill **ski runs** in the Eastern Townships. There are ski tows and a variety of runs and trails. In summer the trails are used by hikers to climb the mountain. A 9 hole golf course has been built in the park, which, like all the Quebec parks, is a game sanctuary.

Thirty miles from Magog, and about two hours' drive from Montreal, there is a summer resort which appeals to us more than a little, and we think you will enjoy its unusual quality, no matter what your tastes may be. It is not on Highway 1, but is ten miles south of it, via **Waterloo**.

Knowlton, on Brome Lake, is one of the most charming places in the Eastern Townships, as many Montrealers and others have found, judging by the size and magnificence of the farms and of the summer colony's houses. The road encircling the lake is pleasant and there are other beautiful drives to the mountains and the scenic Bolton Pass.

Knowlton is a delightful spot for a holiday. The **Golf Club**, facing Brome Lake, has the best 9 hole course we have played for years. You can put up at the club house, if they have a vacancy, and the first tee of the course will be practically under your window. A short distance away is the Boating Club, which helps to make this a top-notch resort. We think the Knowlton Golf Club is the best place to stay, but for non-golfers there are several popular priced **boarding houses and summer inns** around the lake.

The village has a resident **summer theatre**, unique in the fact that it has completed twelve successful seasons. The Brae Manor Playhouse also runs a school of acting, where apprentice players may learn their craft.

An unusual industry has developed at Knowlton. A company called Brome Lake Ducks, Limited breeds trade-marked ducks which are shipped all over the country.

If you are interested in studying the history of the Eastern Townships, you will find the Brome County **Historical Museum** helpful. It is housed in the Paul Holland Knowlton house, commemorating Colonel Knowlton, one of the founders of the village. Among the documents, some of which go back to pre-revolutionary times, is a copy of the letter, dated 1784, to Major Campbell at St. Johns instructing him to remove the Loyalists who had settled at Missisquoi Bay.

Other interesting documents are the account for the expenses incurred by the Government in 1792 in surveying the Townships, and the proclamation of the same year "To such as are desirous to settle on the Lands of the Crown in the Province of Lower Canada". This was the beginning of settlement in the Eastern Townships.

Several roads lead from Knowlton to Montreal. A popular route is along Highway 1, through Granby.

Granby (Population 20,000). This wide-awake city, on a branch of the Yamaska River, has had a remarkable growth during the past twenty-five years, from a comparatively small town to a busy industrial centre with many factories manufacturing textiles, tobacco, rubber and other products. The industrial exhibit in the City Hall on Rue Principale will give you an idea of the extent of the city's manufactured goods. There is a **Tourist Bureau**, also on the Rue Principale, near the Granby and Windsor hotels.

Another attractive drive from Brome Lake to Montreal is through **Cowansville** and **Farnham** on

Highway 40, which crosses and recrosses the Yamaska River. This farming and apple growing country is very pretty in the spring, and here and there you will see a maple sugar bush, always spectacular in the autumn. About 75% of Canada's maple syrup comes from the Eastern Townships.

Because of the many roads, you can tour almost indefinitely in this part of Quebec. Perhaps you may decide to make Knowlton or North Hatley your home for the summer and do that very thing.

It is time, however, for us to leave this area. There are other places and other highways we must tell you about, which have their charm and their interest, too. We shall go first to the north, through the country known as *Les Bois-Francs*—the Hardwood Forests—and then we shall take you to the historic Richelieu River, which no one will want to miss.

Chapter 20

LES BOIS-FRANCS AND THE LAURIER WAY

From Sherbrooke to Quebec
Through Les Bois-Francs

Miles

0	Sherbrooke
24	Richmond - Hy. 22 goes to Drummondville
54	Arthabaska
57	Victoriaville - Hy. 20 goes left to Drummondville
73	Plessisville
82	Laurierville
127	Quebec

ROAD LOG FOR HIGHWAY 9
Sir Wilfrid Laurier Way
From Quebec to Montreal

Miles

0	Quebec (Road under construction)
81	Drummondville
111	St-Hyacinthe
125	Beloeil - Richelieu River
145	Montreal

(While Hy. 9 is under construction use
Hy. 5 to Victoriaville and Hy. 20 from there
to Drummondville)

Les Bois-Francs—THE HARDWOOD FORESTS—which were the curse of the early settlers, have become the glory of the Eastern Townships. Their flaming beauty in the autumn is worth driving miles to see, the sugar and syrup which is made from the maples is famous the country over, and, in recent years, flourishing furniture factories and other forest industries have sprung up in the cities and towns, because of the availability of electric power and wood.

This is new country, as time goes in Quebec. A monument was erected in 1925 to commemorate the one hundredth anniversary of the coming of the first settlers to Les Bois-Francs.

In 1830 the Eastern Townships became acutely road conscious, and the Craig Road was opened to travellers between Richmond and Quebec. Three years later a bill was passed to provide for the repairing and building of roads and bridges in this part of the province. Highway 5 follows, more or less, the old Craig Road.

As you drive north from Sherbrooke, you will pass through **Windsor** and **Richmond**. In spite of their English names and origins, these industrial towns are now predominantly French-speaking.

You will probably want to pause in the town of **Arthabaska** to look at Sir Wilfrid Laurier's house, which has been converted into **a museum** by the Government of the Province of Quebec and which contains some of Sir Wilfrid's own furniture. The museum commemorates Canada's first French Canadian Prime Minister, who headed the government from 1896 until 1911.

Victoriaville (Population 11,000). As its name suggests, this small city was named after the Queen, and it dates only from late Victorian times. In the last twenty-five years it has doubled in size. It is the commercial centre of Les Bois-Francs, and its furniture industry is particularly interesting.

The main street is busy and fairly congested, as this is the junction point for several highways. If you are going directly to Montreal, you take Highway 20. If you are heading for Quebec, you continue on Highway 5, to Plessisville.

Plessisville (Population 5,000). It is easy to tell that this industrial town is in **the maple sugar country**, for there is a co-operative here for *sucre d'érable*, and Plessisville's weekly newspaper is called *La Feuille d'Érable*— The Maple Leaf.

Nine miles farther on you will come to a place which seems to us to be typical of modern French Canadian village life, as opposed to the old habitant settlements of the French regime.

Laurierville (Population 1,000) was incorporated in 1902, and was named in honour of Sir Wilfrid Laurier. The inn at Laurierville is called La Maison Blanche, and we thought the rooms and meals were surprisingly good for such a small place. This inn looks like a private house, and it stands in a pretty garden, with a stable yard where you can park your car. We had drinks on a comfortable, vine-shaded verandah, while we listened to a gramaphone playing Maurice Chevalier records, in French. Across the road, in an enclosed yard, tame deer and Canada geese were wandering about. Next door to us, and towering high above us, was the church of Ste-Julie, its bells a constant reminder that today, as in *Le Vieux Québec*, the Church still rules supreme.

About six miles beyond Laurierville you cross the Rivière-Bécancour at the village of **Lyster**. From there to Quebec the road runs through fertile country, given over mostly to mixed farming.

We had hoped to drive along the new Sir Wilfrid Laurier Highway last summer, on our return trip from Quebec to Montreal, but we found about thirty-five miles or so closed to traffic, and another long stretch still under construction. However, enough of this super-highway had been completed for us to see that it is a fast, multi-lane route which will eventually bring Quebec's two largest cities within about three hours' driving time of each other.

Until the Sir Wilfrid Laurier Way is officially opened to through traffic, you will fare very well by using Highway 5 to Victoriaville and Highway 20 from there to Drummondville. This route is twenty miles longer than the new road will be, but it will always have one advantage. You can see the towns and villages, and you can talk to the people along the way. Our great objection to super-highways is that tourists never stop to see anything, once the speed demon gets into their blood.

Drummondville (Population 25,000). In 1915, one hundred years after the founding of Drummondville by General Heriot and a group of British soldiers, the place was still a village, small and obscure. That year **a power dam** was built on the Rivière-St-François, followed ten years later by another dam and power house. The spectacular growth of Drummondville since that time has turned it into an industrial and commercial city of considerable importance.

The one-hundred-and-fifty-mile-long river, to which the city owes so much, is the same St. Francis River which flows through Sherbrooke. It was a well-known canoe route of the Abenakis, who had a large settlement about twenty miles below Drummondville. This Indian village was the scene of an attack by the Rogers' Rangers in 1759, when it was completely destroyed.

From Drummondville to St-Hyacinthe you follow Highway 9, the Sir Wilfrid Laurier Way. It is straight and very fast, as there are no settlements along it for thirty miles.

St-Hyacinthe (Population 25,000). The flowery name of this industrial city comes from one Hyacinthe Delorme who, in 1753, purchased the seigneurie from Pierre François Rigaud, a brother of the Marquis de Vaudreuil. St-Hyacinthe will celebrate its one hundredth anniversary as a city in 1957. Of all the towns and cities of the Eastern Townships, this is probably the most typically French Canadian, as it is reputed to be 98% French-speaking. It has a number of colleges and schools, among them a unique *École de Textiles*.

The Yamaska River flows through the city, and there are good facilities for sports. We seldom linger long at inland commercial centres, especially in the summer-time, but some people do, and if you are one of these, you will find much of interest in the cities of the Eastern Townships.

The Richelieu River is only fourteen miles from St-Hyacinthe, and remembering its historic past we drove towards it with keen anticipation. Beyond **Ste-Madeleine** an unexpected and isolated mountain seemed to appear from nowhere. It was Mont-St-Hilaire, rising 1,350 feet from an almost flat terrain. It is one of the sisters of Mont-Royal which we had seen from the Lookout in Montreal. The nearby village of **St-Hilaire** is lovely in the spring time when the apple orchards are in bloom, worth coming to see if all around there were nothing but barren wastes.

The Sir Wilfrid Laurier Way crosses the Richelieu River at St-Hilaire and hurries along to Montreal, twenty miles away. Near **St-Lambert**, Highway 9 turns sharply south. Until it reaches the boundary of New York State, it by-passes every settlement and is a speedway to delight the hearts of those who count the success of a trip by the number of miles they can cover in a day.

Go this pace, if you must. For the last lap of our journey we shall be driving, in a leisurely fashion, along the winding roads of the romantic past, as we follow the Richelieu River from Lake Champlain to Sorel.

Chapter 21

DOWN THE RICHELIEU RIVER

FOR MANY PEOPLE WHO COME TO SEE the Richelieu, it is just a pretty river, flowing out of Lake Champlain and following a northerly course for eighty miles, until it empties into the St. Lawrence at Lac St-Pierre.

They glance, in passing, at the **ruins of the old forts**, and they hurry on, making no attempt to reconstruct for themselves the colourful pageant of the centuries as it happened along this highway of history.

It is a beautiful drive, and along it you will meet

again the ghosts of Canadian and American heroes, for every mile of the route has seen some part of the struggle for survival in the New World.

Long before the coming of the French it was the war-path of the Iroquois. These Indians of the Five Nations, who lived in fortified villages along the Mohawk Valley and the Five Finger Lakes, and who hunted in the Adirondacks, came down the Richelieu River to attack the Hurons and the Algonquins who lived north of the St. Lawrence.

At the very beginning of our journey down the river, we meet again the ghost of The Father of New France. While Champlain was spending that first miserable scurvy-haunted winter at his newly-built *habitation* in Lower Town, Quebec, a young Indian chief, from one of the Algonquin tribes, came to ask his aid against the Iroquois. And so, in the summer of 1609, we find Champlain sailing up the Richelieu, which he called the Rivière-des-Algonquins. On this expedition he discovered the lake from which the river flows and gave it his own name—Lac Champlain.

Accompanied by his Indian allies, Champlain sought out the Iroquois. Most of them had never before seen a white man, and, clad in doublet and hose, with a buckled on breastplate, Champlain filled them with fear and amazement.

"When I saw them getting ready to shoot at us with their arrows," he wrote, "I levelled my arquebuse, which I had loaded with four balls, and aimed straight at one of the three chiefs. The shot brought down two, and wounded another."

This first recorded battle of the French against the Iroquois ended in victory for Champlain, but it began the long and terrible conflict which led to such horrors as the massacre of Lachine, and many times threatened to destroy New France.

The first village north of the International boundary line is **Cantic**. Between here and the town of **Lacolle** there is an old blockhouse which saw action in another kind of attack. It helped to defend Canada against American invasion during the War of 1812.

St-Paul-de-l'Ile-aux-Noix is a "must" stop for the historian and an interesting sight for anyone to see. You leave your car in the village and take a row boat to the island, in the middle of the Richelieu River. There you will find **Fort Lennox National Historic Park**. Ile aux Noix belongs to many periods of Canadian and American history. Champlain named the island in 1609, when he passed it on his expedition against the Iroquois. The nut trees have disappeared from Ile aux Noix, probably cut down to clear the way for the fort and parade ground, built in 1759, by order of the French governor, the Marquis de Vaudreuil.

The Chevalier de Bourlamaque was stationed on the Ile aux Noix with 3,500 men to guard against an English attack under General Amherst. Bourlamaque considered the fort impregnable, but it fell to the English the following year. It did not make much difference to the cause of France, as Quebec had already fallen.

Whole regiments of ghosts will rise to greet you on Ile aux Noix. Perhaps you will recognize among them the shades of Rogers and his Rangers who fought there in 1760 and of General Schuyler and General Montgomery, who occupied Fort Lennox in 1775 during the revolt of the English colonists.

The old fort played its part, also, in the American invasion of Canada, during the War of 1812. Many of the present stone buildings date from that time. Although the fort is in a good state of repair, it has a deserted look and a brooding silence hangs over it, as if it were remembering with sadness its almost forgotten past.

Ile aux Noix is only about half a mile long, so it will not take much of your time to look it over, and if you want to know more of its history, the caretaker at Fort Lennox will give you a printed guide.

St-Jean (St. Johns) (Population 18,000). This industrial city was originally settled by soldiers of the Carignan-Salières Regiment which came to America in 1665, sent out by the French government to put an end to the devastating Iroquois raids. Until that time no Frenchman had dared to settle along the Richelieu. The soldiers built a chain of forts on the river which were used first against the Iroquois, then against the English, and finally against the attempted American invasion. The last fort was abandoned as a military post about eighty years ago.

St. Johns gained fame in 1837 as one terminus of the first railroad to be built in Canada. The railway ran to Laprairie, opposite Montreal, and thus connected the water routes of the St. Lawrence with the Richelieu and Lake Champlain.

Across the river from St-Jean, and linked with it by a bridge, is the town of **Iberville**. There is a good road on each side of the river as far as the next bridge, at Chambly-Canton, ten miles downstream.

Chambly (Population 3,500). Here stands a most majestic ruin in **a charming town**. The stone walls of Fort Saint-Louis de Chambly, thirty-five feet high, still present a formidable appearance from the outside, but when we entered through the gate we found that the interior has fallen to destruction and that the wall on the river side is missing. The open square contained within the bastions is now a picturesque park, and **a museum** is housed in the old officers' quarters.

Fort Chambly National Historic Park is the smallest of Canada's twenty-six National Parks, with an area of only two and a half acres, but we think it is one of the most interesting. It has a beautiful site on a point of land in Chambly-Canton, overlooking Chambly Basin.

Captain Jacques de Chambly, who gave the fort and the town his name, must have been a man of courage and enterprise. He came to Canada in 1665 with the famous Carignan Regiment, to subdue the Iroquois. When his regiment returned to France, three years later, Chambly and many of the other officers and soldiers decided to remain in Canada. Chambly was granted the seigneurie around Fort St-Louis, and he remained there for eight years. When he left the Richelieu Valley, it was to become commandant of Acadia, and later Governor of Grenada and of Martinique, in the French West Indies.

The first Fort St-Louis de Chambly was built of palisades, fifteen feet high. It enclosed the barracks, a chapel and a storehouse. Albanel, the Jesuit explorer of Lac St-Jean and Hudson's Bay, was chaplain of the fort at Chambly in 1666. Dollier de Casson visited it from Ville-Marie, twenty miles away. It was a place of great importance in its day.

The stone fort, which now makes such a beautiful ruin, was built in 1710 and was pronounced to be "good and sound enough to last forever". We hope that it may, for it seems to us that it is a unifying link between the French, the English and the Americans. Each has a stake in its past, as each in turn occupied it—the

French, before they became Canadians; the English, before they divided into Canadians and Americans; and the Americans, once the division was complete.

Chambly has a Club de Golf, and some fine stretches of river for boating, including a canal, built here to overcome the rapids.

In recent times, the town had a famous singer who will long be remembered, mostly because of Drummond's poem about her, *When Albani Sang*.

> But no matter de moch she enjoy it, for travel
>   all roun' de worl',
> Somet'ing on de heart bring her back here, for
>   she was de Chambly girl.

"Somet'ing on de heart" brings us back there, too, whenever we are in the vicinity of Montreal, for Chambly is a rare place that fosters history, and memories and dreams.

Continuing down the river, you cross the bridge to **Richelieu** and stay on the right bank the rest of the way. The road goes through the village of **St-Mathias**, where Ethan Allen and his Green Mountain Boys camped during the American Revolution, and brings you once again to **St-Hilaire**.

Beloeil (Population 2,500) is across the river. When we were there in July, it was hot and still, and the river was gay with people swimming, and with motor boats running up and down at top speed. There are some delightful summer cottages along the shores, and some lovely old houses in the town. The unexpected mountains rising from the plain give interest to the landscape. Below St-Hilaire, **ferries** cross the river at St-Charles, St-Denis and St-Ours, but there is not another bridge until you

(*Above*) FORT CHAMBLY ON THE RICHELIEU RIVER
(*Below*) THE HOTEL AT LAURIERVILLE LOOKS LIKE A PRIVATE HOUSE

come to Sorel, at the river's mouth, thirty-five miles away.

We have come to the end of the Richelieu River and we are very close to the end of our tour of the province. Before we part we would like to show you the sites of some of the seigneuries of the French regime, established mostly by the brother officers of Jacques de Chambly who remained in Canada when the Carignan-Salières Regiment went back to France.

If this does not tempt you, or if you are in a great hurry to get to Montreal, you can take a short cut from Chambly on Highway 1, or from Beloeil on Highway 9, and you will be in the city in about half an hour.

Chapter 22

BACK TO MONTREAL AND AU REVOIR

ROAD LOG FOR HIGHWAY 3
From Sorel to Montreal

Miles

0	Sorel - St. Lawrence River
16	Contrecoeur
24	Verchères
31	Varennes
36	Boucherville
41	Longueuil
47	Montreal

THE LAST LAP OF OUR JOURNEY begins at a point where the Richelieu and the St. Lawrence Rivers meet, where Champlain camped in 1609, and where Fort Richelieu was built, in 1665, as a protection against the Iroquois.

Sorel (Population 18,000). The city was named for Captain Pierre Saurel, one of Chambly's brother officers, who helped to build the fort and who became the military seigneur of the surrounding country.

Sorel is typical of Quebec's rapidly expanding industrial development. Although its roots are deep in the history of the province, it seems to belong to the twentieth century, and it possesses the faults as well as the virtues of this modern age of industry and commerce. It is a place to visit if you are interested in marine construction, or in the new metal, **titanium**, which is processed in the recently completed electric furnaces of the Sorel smelters.

The road from Sorel to Montreal is interesting and picturesque. It runs close to the St. Lawrence River most of the way and passes through three of the old military seigneuries. They still bear the names of the officers of the Carignan Regiment who founded them, Contrecoeur, Verchères and Varennes.

The military seigneur was usually a gallant but penniless officer. He owned little but the land given him for his services and the money paid him by the king for getting married. Chambly and Saurel fared the best, as their land surrounded strong forts already built to protect them. Each of the others had to build his own fort as well as his house, a chapel and a mill. His tenants were the disbanded soldiers from the regiment.

Verchères is probably the most interesting of this group of old seigneuries, and the one most often visited, not because of the seigneur, but because of his daughter, Madeleine de Verchères. Much of the early history of Canada was never recorded and has been lost, but the familiar story of how Madeleine defended her father's fort for a week against Iroquois attack was saved for the history books by the Marquis de Beauharnois, Governor of Canada. Beauharnois had the story of the defence of Verchères written down, exactly as it happened in 1692, dictated by Madeleine herself.

The old fort and the blockhouse have gone, but on their site, overlooking the river in the quiet village of Verchères, **an impressive statue has been erected**. It depicts Madeleine as a girl of fourteen, standing defiantly, courageously, gun in hand, ready to meet any fate.

Years later, as a woman of twenty-eight, Madeleine married one Pierre-Thomas Tarieu de la Pérade. She went to live across the river, below Trois-Rivières, in her husband's village of Ste-Anne-de-la-Pérade, where she is reputed to have become involved in innumerable law suits, and where she died in her seventieth year.

Varennes is the next military seigneurie. It is eight miles up the river from Verchères, and like most of these earliest settlements, it is linked inseparably with the great names of Canadian history.

A letter written in 1667 by the Intendant Talon to King Louis' minister, carried the news that a lieutenant of the Carignan-Salières Regiment had married a daughter of the Governor of Trois-Rivières. The bride was twelve year old Marie Bochart, and the lieutenant was René Gaultier, who had been granted the seigneurie of Varennes the previous year.

This René Gaultier de Varennes later moved to Trois-Rivières, where he became the governor, and where a son was born in 1685. The son grew up to be the famous explorer, Pierre Gaultier de Varennes, Sieur de La Vérendrye.

Varennes has not grown much through the years, and many of the old houses of the French regime are still standing. The charming manor house at 100 Rue Ste-Anne was built in 1723. Near it, on the breakwater, a statue commemorates the 250th anniversary of the founding of the Parish of Varennes, in 1693, just one year after Madeleine's defence of Verchères.

Boucherville (Population 2,000) is another famous old town which dates from 1668. It was granted as a seigneurie to the renowned Pierre Boucher, in 1672. Pierre, you may remember, was one of the boys who lived among

the Indians to learn their language. He became the first
interpreter at Trois-Rivières and then its governor, at
which time he was given the seigneurie of Yamachiche.
As a reward for saving Trois-Rivières from an Indian
attack, he was also granted the seigneurie of Boucherville. Pierre built the manor house and retired there in
1668 to write his interesting history of Canada, which
bears the cumbersome title of *Histoire Véritable et
Naturelle des Moeurs et des Productions de la Nouvelle-
France.*

The village has great charm, with its lovely old
French houses. The Boucherville Islands squat in the
river in front of it, and beyond you can see the metro-
politan area of Montreal. The heart of the city is only
eleven miles away.

Pierre Boucher of Boucherville lived about half-way
between the seigneurie of René Gaultier of Varennes and
that of Charles Le Moyne at Longueuil. Unfortunately
the Le Moyne Seigneurie, the oldest and greatest of
them all, is no longer standing.

Across the Jacques Cartier Bridge from Longueuil,
lies the city of Montreal, where we must say good-by.

We have come a long way together, in miles and in
time. We have travelled by road approximately 3,800
miles, and we have glimpsed something of the history of
the past four hundred years. Jacques Cartier's cross at
Gaspé is more than four centuries away from St. Joseph's
Shrine on Westmount, and the birds of Bonaventure are
a thousand miles from the smelters of Noranda-Rouyn.

Those are great distances to cover, mentally and
physically, and we hope we have not hurried you too
unceremoniously from one place to another, and from
one century to the next. Unfortunately one can never

travel in chronological order. Highways are not laid out that way.

We think that Quebec is unique. It has a glorious past and a tremendous future. If we have helped you to visualize these things and, at the same time, to enjoy its unusually delightful present, we are content.

Au revoir and happy holidays, until we meet again.

INDEX

INDEX TO HOTELS, RESORTS, AND RESTAURANTS

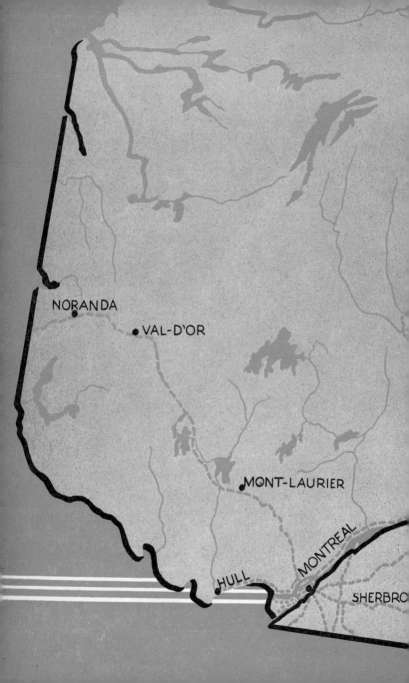